W9-ANZ-570

DRAMATISTS PLAY SERVICE

OUTSTANDING WOMEN'S MONOLOGUES 2001–2002

Edited by CRAIG POSPISIL

★

DRAMATISTS
PLAY SERVICE
INC.

OUTSTANDING WOMEN'S MONOLOGUES 2001–2002
Copyright © 2002, Dramatists Play Service, Inc.

All Rights Reserved

INTRODUCTION

There has been a proliferation of monologue collections in recent years. Browse through the theatre section of any bookstore and you will find collections of dramatic monologues, comic ones, classical ones; monologues written by men, by women, by gay writers, Asian-American writers, African-American writers, the best monologues of 1998, 1999, 2000 … you get the idea.

What I noticed was that most of these collections featured the work of authors published by Dramatists Play Service, and so the idea came to me, "Why not a monologue collection drawn solely from plays that we publish?" After all, we represent some of the best of today's playwrights, authors who in the last eight years have won six Pulitzer Prizes and six Tony Awards, authors whose work is produced all across North America and the world, and writers of every stripe and style.

I read through all of the plays that we published in the last couple of seasons and compiled two collections: *Outstanding Men's Monologues 2001–2002* and *Outstanding Women's Monologues 2001–2002*. Each of these books contains over fifty monologues. You will find an enormous range of voices and subject matter, characters from their teens to their seventies and authors from widely varied backgrounds, some well known, others less so, but all immensely talented.

I hope this collection will prove useful to you in your search for audition material, classroom work or just for reading pleasure. Perhaps you'll be introduced to some new authors as well. I know you'll find some very exciting writing for the theatre in these pages.

Craig Pospisil
New York City
October 2001

3

CONTENTS

4

5

APARTMENT 3A

BY JEFF DANIELS

ANNIE — 30s.

SYNOPSIS: Reeling from the loss of what she thought was the love of her life, Annie Wilson, an executive at her local PBS channel, searches for a reason to hope again with a mysterious next-door neighbor, who teaches her what it truly means to be in love forever.

ANNIE.   *(To unseen camera.)* Welcome. Welcome and hello. My name is Annie Wilson and I'm WPBK's Director of Fundraising here at Channel 68. Before we go back to Big Bird and all of his wonderful friends on *Sesame Street*, we're going to take a short little break for just a couple minutes, because we have to do something that's very, very important. How many Big Bird fans do we have out there? Let me see you raise your hands? Oh, my! So many of you! That's great. Y'know, Big Bird and his friends like you just as much as you like them and I know all of my friends behind me love Big Bird and all of his friends, too. Don't you? Yes, indeed. But unfortunately, bringing *Sesame Street* into your home costs money. And that's why we're here. Channel 68 needs your help. If there are any of you parents out there who are watching *Sesame Street* along with your children, you may have noticed there are no commercials on public broadcasting. Instead of selling advertising spots that would break up our programming, we rely on the help of you, our viewers, big and small. That's why these wonderful people are behind me poised over their telephones. They are waiting for you to pick up your phone and make a donation that will make sure Big Bird and all his friends on *Sesame Street* can keep coming into your home every morning. Because if they couldn't ... if they couldn't that would be ... that would be bad. B-A-D, bad, boys and girls. Because ... okay. All right. Here it is. You know what's going to happen if no one calls? Do you have any idea what will happen if those phones don't ring? There will be no more *Sesame Street*. And no more *Sesame Street* means no Big Bird. No Bert and Ernie. No Oscar. No Cookie Monster. No Mr. Snuffleupagus. All of your friends on *Sesame Street* will be gone. That's what will happen, boys and girls, if those phones don't ring. Because without Channel 68, Big Bird and all of his friends will be dead. And ... you know what dead is, don't you, boys and girls? Dead is gone. Dead is — *(Phones start ringing.)* — goodbye. Dead is someplace you don't want to go. Someplace you don't want to be. Something you wouldn't wish on anyone. Except for certain right-wing extremists on Capitol Hill who think public television isn't worthy of federal funding and military bands are. *(The sound of many phones ringing.)* Are those phones I hear ringing? Why, I think they are. But wait, I think I still see a few of you boys and girls just sitting there. Don't be shy. Just walk over, pick up your phone and call us at 1-800-555-WPBK. And if you're too young to dial the number yourself, don't cry. Just go get one of your parents and tell them, "Please, Mommy and Daddy. Help save Big Bird. Call Channel 68 and make a pledge. Before it's too late." *(Annie holds a smile.)*

THE BATTING CAGE

BY JOAN ACKERMANN

JULIANNA — 40.

SYNOPSIS: In a Holiday Inn in romantic St. Augustine, Florida, two estranged sisters travel unlikely journeys as they struggle to regain their bearings after the loss of their much-loved third sister. Julianna talks, Wilson doesn't. Their efforts at redefining themselves and their relationship are both poignant and humorous. A dashing conquistador, a lost suitcase, a bellhop with a barnacle growing in his ear are but a few of the many surprising turns in this unusual and very moving story.

JULIANNA. One question. Do you have … any idea … what it is like to be so lonely, so lonely that you actually look forward to going to the dentist just for the pleasure of feeling a man's hand, anyone's hand, pressed against your face?
[WILSON. Julianna …](During the following, Julianna sits up very slowly, painstakingly.)
JULIANNA. So lonely that even a visit to a novice acupuncturist is something to be looked forward to. To be pleasantly anticipated, the chance to spend time with a person who is so inept at sticking needles into your body that he misses the points he is aiming for and has to stick them in again and again, hurting you over and over? Do you know how *lonely* it is to go on vacation with a sister who won't talk to you or be seen in public with you? To go off on your own to inane tourist attractions where you have to listen to the sound of lethargic disgusting fat alligators crunching on the bones of large species of muskrat at feeding time? To sit on a tour bus *alone* while everyone else is sharing, talking, pointing out historic landmarks, laughing? To lie sun-

9

burnt in bed, burnt to a crisp, and hear your sister talking for the first time in a week, describe to you in panoramic epic detail how she had an orgasm in a giant cage in front of a cheering crowd? Wilson? I'm speechless.

THE BEAUTY QUEEN OF LEENANE

BY MARTIN McDONAGH

MAUREEN — 40, plain and slim.

SYNOPSIS: Set in the mountains of Connemara, County Galway, THE BEAUTY QUEEN OF LEENANE tells the darkly comic tale of Maureen Folan, a plain and lonely woman, and Mag, her manipulative aging mother, whose interference in Maureen's first and possibly final chance of a loving relationship sets in motion a train of events that leads inexorably towards the play's terrifying dénouement in which Maureen, poker in hand, confronts Mag in her rocking chair.

MAUREEN. To Boston. To Boston I'll be going. Isn't that where them two were from, the Kennedys, or was that somewhere else, now? Robert Kennedy I did prefer over Jack Kennedy. He seemed to be nicer to women. Although I haven't read up on it. *(Pause.)* Boston. It does have a nice ring to it. Better than England it'll be, I'm sure. Although where wouldn't be better than England? No shite I'll be cleaning there, anyways, and no names called, and Pato'll be there to have a say-so anyways if there was to be names called, but I'm sure there won't be. The Yanks do love the Irish. *(Pause.)* Almost begged me, Pato did. Almost on his hands and knees, he was, near enough crying. At the station I caught him, not five minutes to spare, thanks to you. Thanks to your oul interfering. But too late to be interfering you are now. Oh aye. Be far too late, although you did give it a good go, I'll say that for you. Another five minutes and you'd have had it. Poor you. Poor selfish oul bitch, oul you. *(Pause.)* Kissed the face off me, he did, when he saw me there. Them blue eyes of his. Them muscles. Them

11

arms wrapping me. "Why did you not answer me letter?" And all for coming over and giving you a good kick he was when I told him, but "Ah no," I said, "isn't she just a feeble-minded oul feck, not worth dirtying your boots on?" I was defending you there. *(Pause.)* "You will come to Boston with me so, me love, when you get up the money." "I will, Pato. Be it married or be it living in sin, what do I care? What do I care if tongues'd be wagging? Tongues have wagged about me before, let them wag again. Let them never stop wagging, so long as I'm with you, Pato, what do I care about tongues? So long as it's you and me, and the warmth of us cuddled up, and the skins of us asleep, is all I ever really wanted anyway." *(Pause.)* "Except we do still have a problem, what to do with your oul mam, there," he said. "Would an oul folks home be too harsh?" "It wouldn't be too harsh but it would be too expensive." "What about your sisters so?" "Me sisters wouldn't have the bitch. Not even a half-day at Christmas to be with her can them two stand. They clear forgot her birthday this year as well as that. 'How do you stick her without going off your rocker?' they do say to me. Behind her back, like." *(Pause.)* "I'll leave it up to yourself so," Pato says. He was on the train be this time, we was kissing out the window, like they do in films. "I'll leave it up to yourself so, whatever you decide. If it takes a month, let it take a month. And if it's finally you decide you can't bear to be parted from her and have to stay behind, well, I can't say I would like it, but I'd understand. But if even a year it has to take for you to decide, it is a year I will be waiting, and won't be minding the wait." "It won't be a year it is you'll be waiting, Pato," I called out then, the train was pulling away. "It won't be a year nor yet nearly a year. It won't be a week!" *(The rocking-chair has stopped its motions. Mag starts to slowly lean forward at the waist until she finally topples over and falls heavily to the floor, dead. A red chunk of skull hangs from a string of skin at the side of her head. Maureen looks down at her, somewhat bored, taps her on the side with the toe of her shoe, then steps onto her back and stands there in thoughtful contemplation.)* 'Twas over the stile she did trip. Aye. And down the hill she did fall. Aye. *(Pause.)* Aye.

BETTY'S SUMMER VACATION

BY CHRISTOPHER DURANG

BETTY — a nice, fairly normal young woman, late 20s. Sensible, does her best to be reasonable.

SYNOPSIS: Betty is looking forward to her summer share at the ocean. But her housemate, Trudy, whom she knows only slightly, chatters incessantly; and then there are the other housemates — sexy lout Buck, who's pathologically on the make with women all the time, and sweet, withdrawn Keith who carries a shovel and a mysterious hatbox and just may be a serial killer. Then the emotionally anarchic landlady, Mrs. Siezmagraff, moves in too; and she invites a crazy derelict to dinner, and, well, the vacation becomes more and more of a strain for poor Betty. Not to mention there seems to be a laugh track coming from the ceiling that no one seems able to shut up. The play builds to a murderous end, and Betty flees to the beach just as the house explodes.

BETTY. […] I think I'd like to become a hermit. Or I might become a nun if I could live in a convent in an isolated area with no other people around, and where no one in the convent is allowed to speak ever. I'd like that if it was quiet, and peaceful, and if they didn't care if I believed in God or not. *(Another idea.)* Or maybe I could start my own community where people don't speak. And we'd plant our own food, and we'd watch the birds in the trees. And maybe I'm having a breakdown. *(Holds the sides of her head, as if it might fly apart.)* Or is it a breakthrough? *(Hop another possibility.)* Maybe it's a bad dream I had, and am stil' ing. *(Looks around her.)* But I seem to be on the beach. A house seems to be smoldering somewhere behind me in tance. *(Looks behind her; the glow is almost out now; the sound of explosions has stopped; we hear the sound of the ocean.)* Isn't the sound of the ocean wonderful? *(Calming down slightly.)* What is it about it that sounds so wonderful? But it does. It makes me feel good. It makes me feel connected. *(Realizing what she said before was a little off.)* Well, maybe I don't have to join a convent where they don't speak. Maybe that's overreacting. But it is hard to be around civilization. I don't like people. But there are nice people, though, aren't there? Yes. I'm sure you're very nice — although I'm just trying to ingratiate myself to you so you don't try to cut any of my body parts off. *(Laughs, then cries.)* Now I'm sad. *(Suddenly looks up, scared.)* Now I'm frightened. *(The emotions pass.)* No, now I'm fine. Listen to the ocean. That's why I wanted to come on this vacation, and have a summer share at the beach. I wanted to hear the ocean. But you know I forgot to listen to it the whole time I was with those people. But I'm going to listen to it now. *(Listens; she and the audience hear the sound of the waves; tension leaves Betty's face and body.)* Oh that's lovely. Yes. Ocean, waves, sand. I'm starting to feel better.

BLUES FOR AN ALABAMA SKY

BY PEARL CLEAGE

ANGEL ALLEN — a 34-year-old black woman who looks five years younger; former back-up singer at the Cotton Club.

SYNOPSIS: It is the summer of 1930 in Harlem, New York. The creative euphoria of the Harlem Renaissance has given way to the harsher realities of the Great Depression. The play brings together a rich cast of characters who reflect the conflicting currents of the time through their overlapping personalities and politics. Set in the Harlem apartment of Guy, a popular costume designer, and his friend, Angel, a recently fired Cotton Club back-up singer, the cast also includes Sam, a hard-working, jazz-loving doctor at Harlem Hospital; Delia, an equally dedicated member of the staff at the Sanger clinic; and Leland, a recent transplant from Tuskegee, who sees in Angel a memory of lost love and a reminder of those "Alabama skies where the stars are so thick it's bright as day." But Angel doesn't want to be Leland's dream.

ANGEL. Tony T. called the guys and told them the audition was cancelled so when I got there, the place was empty. It was just me and him. So he says they must be caught in traffic or something and offers me a drink while we're waiting and right then, just that quick, I felt it.
[LELAND. Felt what?]
ANGEL. The truth of it. My trying to play headliner. Guy trying to play Paris. The whole truth of it. Tony kept saying he could look out for me. Offer me some protection in these hard times. *(A beat.)* He didn't want a singer any more than you do. He wanted to keep a colored woman stashed up in Harlem so he could come

by every now and then and rub her head for luck.

[LELAND. That son of a ... (He reaches for her protectively.)
ANGEL. Don't.
LELAND. No Negro woman should have to ...]*

ANGEL. No Negro woman should have to anything, and so what? Do you even understand what I'm talking about? When I was sitting there at Tony's this afternoon, I saw him looking like he could see right through my clothes, and I knew he had talked to Nick about me. I didn't have to imagine what they said. I've heard them talk about women. I know what they say. But I wouldn't let myself think about that. I pushed it right on out of my mind because I know how to take care of myself! I'm not going to be a broke old woman, begging up and down 125th Street, dreaming about fine clothes and French champagne. So, I drank with him and listened to him telling me how long he'd been wanting to get to know me better and I watched him put his hand on my knee like I wouldn't notice and I pretended not to. And I laughed and laughed just to keep up some noise in that room. It was so quiet ... Then I stood up to pour another drink and I saw myself in the mirror ... and I thought what is that poor, crazy, colored woman laughing about? *(A beat.)* When I turned around, there was Tony, waiting for his answer, so I gave it to him ...

BOOK OF DAYS

BY LANFORD WILSON

MARTHA HOCH — around 50, brilliant and fun. Len's mother; junior college dean and teacher.

SYNOPSIS: All seems right in Dublin, Missouri. Ruth Hoch has just been cast as the lead in the local production of St. Joan, and she has her hands full between memorizing her lines and her bookkeeping job. She relies on Len, her husband, and Martha, her iconoclastic mother-in-law, for support. But when Ruth's boss, and Dublin's most prominent citizen, dies in a hunting accident, she senses that something isn't right. The story that Earl tells about the night of the accident has too many loose ends, and Ruth cannot stop pulling at the threads even though it may turn the whole town against her.

MARTHA. I can't for the life of me understand what the hell is going on with these kids today, I just saw a girl walking out of the pharmacy with her body pierced and stapled in every possible — rows of silver rings and studs through her lip, her cheek, her eyebrow, on her neck, her nose, her belly button — you know damn well she's got one on her clit.
[LEN. Mom.]
MARTHA. I'd like to see her drop *that* in the dish at airport security.
[RUTH. I know. I don't get it at all.]
MARTHA. And I'll bet you a dollar she'll be in my Freshman English Composition class this fall.
[LEN. They're just trying to express their individuality.]
MARTHA. Yeah, individuality and license. Let freedom ring. God above. Still they're not as bad as — I swear half my kids don't know they're alive. They live a calm, sexless denial of every human

17

impulse. Passionless, humorless little automatons. What is that? In the '60s we — well the late '60s, we rejoiced in our bodies. I don't mind them raising hell at that age, but the option now seems to be between self-mutilation and total denial of your existence.
[RUTH.   I don't get it.]
MARTHA.   (Mocking.) And after all the indiscriminate sex and the endless ingestion of drugs we endured to set them free. We didn't put ourselves through those perilous experiments for ourselves. We did it for them. For our children. And our children's children. (Pokes Ruth.)
[RUTH.   I heard that.]
MARTHA.   Good. Slopping barefoot and naked through the rain and mud at Woodstock. For what? To make our country free! Liberation! And look at what the Perforated Generation has done with it. I've got to get myself another story. I have thoroughly worn out Woodstock, haven't I?

COLLECTED STORIES

BY DONALD MARGULIES

RUTH — late 50s.

SYNOPSIS: Lisa Morrison is a young writer, studying with Ruth Steiner, a famous author of short stories. Ruth is a formidable and opinionated woman, and Lisa is awed by her and soaks up everything she says. As the years pass, the two women grow close and Lisa's writing begins to meet with some success. But when Lisa's first novel is accepted for publication Ruth is enraged. Lisa based her novel on Ruth's life and especially on her youthful affair with the difficult, alcoholic poet Delmore Schwartz. Ruth insists that Lisa withdraw the book or she will sue. Lisa protests that she has only done what all writers do, what Ruth herself taught her to do, to collect stories and experiences and transform them into art. But Ruth refuses to listen or forgive her, and their relationship is forever shattered.

RUTH. I'd just come to the city from Detroit, to be a poet, of course, and took an apartment, a tiny walk-up, on Grove Street, above an Italian restaurant. The place smelled of garlic. Always. It was wonderful. My pillow smelled of garlic, my clothes. I had a roommate named Elaine, who was also from Detroit, the daughter of a friend of a family friend and an aspiring actress who would soon marry a rich man and give up her dream forever and die of breast cancer at thirty-nine, and the only soul I knew in all of New York City. *(A beat.)* One sleeting night, Elaine shlepped me into a bar on Hudson Street — The White Horse Tavern — and there, sitting in a booth, his wide handsome moon face shining, his big voice booming for all to hear whether they liked it or not ... There, performing for the two adoring pretty coeds who sat at his table ... There, was the great poet Delmore Schwartz, mad

prophet, squandered genius, son of "Europe, America and Israel."
[LISA. Oh, Ruth, this is incredible.]
RUTH. We sat across the aisle, Elaine and I, and he included us in his rant, I don't know, about DiMaggio one minute, Kierkegaard the next. After midnight, the first team of cheerleaders grew tired and left, and Elaine and I moved our drinks into his booth. Seeing his shining face across the table now, his eyes darting about, gleaming with brilliance ... There was so much going *on* in there. And he was already way past his prime at this point. He was gray and bloated and going to seed. His overcoat reeked of stale smoke and his teeth were baked yellow from tobacco. That enormous head with those widely-spaced eyes. There was still something magnificent about him. He had been quite beautiful, once.
[LISA. I know, I've seen pictures.]
RUTH. So, yes, the power was undeniable. *(A beat.)* He was only forty-four but there was something ancient about him, something terribly mortal and immortal at the same time, if that makes any sense. He seemed to possess so much wisdom and yet, even then, even that first sleeting night, he seemed doomed. *(A beat.)* What sheltered Jewish girl from Detroit, what self-styled poet, what virgin, would *not* have succumbed?

THE COUNTRY CLUB

BY DOUGLAS CARTER BEANE

CHLOE — full name: Chloe Maria Donna DeGlatalia. Beautiful. Her Mediterranean looks are a direct contrast to the Anglo-Saxons. So is her matter-of-fact directness. A slight South Philadelphia dialect. She is newly married to Hutch.

SYNOPSIS: Soos, young, witty and charmingly neurotic, retreats from a failed marriage to her upper-class hometown. The type of WASP domain with the houses "that made Martha Stewart forget she was Polish." As party after party unfolds, the getaway weekend gives way to a year, and ultimately the rest of her life. Brittle conversation is bandied about, and Soos is reunited with her onetime boyfriend, the ever charming Zip. She also returns to her circle of old friends: the highly strung party planner Froggy, the wry and sarcastic Pooker and the drunken good ol' boy Hutch. But cracks soon begin to show in the veneer. Zip falls in and out of an easy relationship with Soos. He starts an affair with Chloe. They soon discover, however, that the affair is widely known even if not widely talked about. Lives are casually destroyed and lives go on.

CHLOE.   And all my friends, my friends back on Reed Street, they ask me, "What's it like at the country club with all those country club snobs who got no heart and got no soul?" And I say, "No they're fine, they're just like you or me." *(Her words build in exhilaration.)* But the truth, the fucking truth, is you ain't, you people ain't like anybody, you got no soul, you got no heart, you got no God, no hell, no saints, no sin, no wrong, no sin, *(With each "no," she strikes Zip.)* no pain, no Jesus, no Mother of Jesus, no sin, no guilt, no hell, no hell, no hell. I hate you. *(She cries. He goes to comfort. She steps away and regains her composure.)* That's it. No. I mean, this is it. It is over as of this second.

[ZIP. I —]

CHLOE. Don't try. It's a waste of breath. It went on too long as is. Now everyone knows. Or to be more exact now we know that everyone knows. God only knows how long they've known or how long Hutch has known. *(It dawns on her what she has just said. She looks scared. She begins to cry.)* Oh God.

[ZIP. *Shit. Don't cry. (He goes to comfort her. She moves away. She starts to leave, but stops at the door. She doesn't look at him.)]*

CHLOE. I'm not crying. No one is going to see me cry.

COYOTE ON A FENCE

BY BRUCE GRAHAM

SHAWNA DuCHAMPS — a prison guard, Shawna is a solid-looking woman, but tired and washed-out.

SYNOPSIS: Illiterate but likable, Bobby Reyburn is a funny young guy who loves to do impressions. He's also a member of the Aryan nation, a racist predator convicted of a horrific crime. John Brennan is educated and arrogant, a serious writer who may only be guilty of doing society a favor. Sam Fried is a reporter who is writing an article on John for the New York Times. *As he interviews people at the prison, he challenges John's claim of innocence and shows that the divide between John and Bobby may not be so great after all.*

SHAWNA. Usta be — 'fore they switched to the needle — when we still had the chair? — the lights would dim. No shit — just like in them old Bogart movies, they'd go ... *(She illustrates.)* Zzzzzzzzzzzzz ... then come back up. That's 'cause they were workin' off the prison generator 'cause — and this is such bull-shit — the electric company didn't wanta be ... fuck, what's the word — you better quit feedin' me drinks — they didn't want nothin' to do with it, and they — PARTICIPANT — that's it — that's the word — they didn't wanta be a participants in an exe-cution. Is that bullshit or what — packa fuckin' thieves like the 'lectric company gettin' all righteous. I mean, I don't know what you pay, but my bill ... fuckin' thieves. Hypocrites — 'cause they're all for it — hell, everybody 'round here's for it 'cept for a couple of them crazies out front with their goddamn candles and their ... like we enjoy this, right? *(Loses her train of thought.)* Fucking electric company! They want guys executed but don't

23

want people thinkin' they're responsible — like they're gonna boycott the product or somethin'. We're not talkin' 'bout sneakers or … beer or somethin'. It's the 'lectric company, they got ya by the balls and they know it.

THE DIARY OF ANNE FRANK

BY FRANCES GOODRICH AND ALBERT HACKETT

NEWLY ADAPTED BY WENDY KESSELMAN

ANNE FRANK — 14.

SYNOPSIS: It is World War II and Amsterdam has fallen to the Nazi regime. Seeking refuge in a forgotten storage attic, Otto and Edith Frank try to maintain a sense of security and hope for their daughters, Margot and Anne. With limited supplies, they agree to hide another family, the van Daans, and a dentist, Mr. Dussel. Days become months as tensions mount and news reports worsen. Anne, a gifted young girl of fourteen, records the daily events in her diary. Her accounts are filled with the humor, pain and passion of a young girl becoming a woman. She tries to maintain her belief in the general goodness of humanity, but as her world and traditions are destroyed, her optimism fades. The families survive bitter winters, malnutrition and volatile relationships, but they are ultimately captured.

ANNE.   Sometimes I see myself alone in a dungeon, without Father and Mother, or I'm roaming the streets, or the Annex is on fire, or they come in the middle of the night to take us away, and I know it could all happen soon. I see the eight of us in the Annex as if we were a patch of blue sky surrounded by menacing black clouds. The perfectly round spot on which we stand is still safe, but the clouds are moving in on us, and the ring between us and the approaching danger is being pulled tighter and tighter. We're surrounded by darkness and danger, and in our desperate search for a way out we keep bumping into each other.

We look at the fighting down below and the peace and beauty above, but we're cut off by the dark mass of clouds and can go neither up nor down. It looms before us, an impenetrable wall, trying to crush us, but not yet able to. I can only cry out and implore, "Oh ring, ring, open wide and let us out!"

DIMLY PERCEIVED THREATS TO THE SYSTEM

BY JON KLEIN

CHRISTINE — 13, Josh and Maryls' daughter.

SYNOPSIS: Maryls Hauser is a management consultant who can't seem to manage the slightest problem at home. Her husband, Josh, is developing a film about the American Family in Crisis — while slipping into an affair with his own producer. Their comically dysfunctional daughter, Christine, torments her school therapist — when she's not channeling the spirit of her grandmother. Reality and fantasy overlap with hilarious results as this unforgettable family attempts to survive the nineties.

CHRISTINE.   So I'm in this room full of people I hate.
[MR. SYKES.   I take it this is a big room.]
CHRISTINE.   Like a train station. There's Mr. Mosley, who asked me if I had attention deficit disorder — right in front of the whole class. And Mrs. Shank, who said I should make more of an effort to look feminine. And Paula Rieger, who taped pictures of raw meat to my locker. And Bobby Lacone, who said I have no tits. So I start with Bobby. See, I've got this huge bucket full of bugs —
[MR. SYKES.   Bugs?]
CHRISTINE.   Yeah, like worms and slugs and black widow spiders and poisonous centipedes, and I'm trying to pour it all down his throat. I mean, he's all tied up and everything, so it shouldn't be too hard, but he keeps his mouth closed tight. Then Jesus floats down from heaven, right through the ceiling, and all these rain-

27

bows appear and cool trumpet music plays, and he looks at me and says, in this really deep and mysterious voice, "You seem troubled, my child." And Jesus grabs Bobby's head and forces his mouth open so I can pour, and before you know it he's got bugs crawling out his nose and ears, and stinging his eyeballs, and his head blows up to the size of a watermelon, and ...

[...]

CHRISTINE.   *[...]* You think it's bad, don't you?

[MR. SYKES.   Absolutely not. It's completely normal for a girl your age to have revenge fantasies.]

CHRISTINE.   It's not a fantasy. It's a story. For class.

DREAMTIME FOR ALICE

BY SUSAN KIM

ALICE — an upper-middle-class, educated, white or Asian woman in her mid-40s. She is brittle, assured and glib on the surface, and full of rage, fear and mollusk vulnerability underneath. She is hatless, in shorts, sandals, T-shirt and blouse.

SYNOPSIS: Book editor Alice flees a failed marriage and suburban despair in America and finds herself unintentionally stranded in the Australian outback. Armed with only sunscreen, a Swiss army knife and a caustic attitude, she is initially breezy. However, she grows increasingly desperate and watches both self-assurance and her very worldview slip away as she begins to question not only the possibility of rescue, but the deeper meaning of her life. By finally owning up to her weaknesses and asking for grace, she is able to attain a certain transcendence ... but at a cost.

ALICE. Jesus God in heaven, thank you, thank you Mother Mary, Mama's goin' home ... *(She jumps up and runs downstage, waving.)* Hello! Over here! Hellooo! *(She slowly stops. She squints, rubbing her eyes. She laughs.)*

Well, talk about dubious accomplishments — I've had my first hallucination. But Jesus Christ, I could have sworn ...

I'm not religious, by the way. I know I mention God and Christ an awful lot, it may even look like I'm trying to petition them, but believe me, I'm not. The words just blip out of me sometimes, like ... religious Tourette's. Of course if your parents dragged you to church every Sunday for eighteen years, you'd know what I was talking about. It imprints on your brain in a very sinister way. Part of it always stays with you, like a vestigial ... flipper. Actually, that's not completely true, is it?

I can honestly say I don't believe in God, and never did ... but wasn't there a time I was willing to give him a chance? What was I, eleven? Twelve? I had this friend, Mary. Mary Chaney. She went to Quaker meeting every Sunday with her family, and one day she asked if I wanted to go with them. So I did, and the only thing I remember was that this really old guy, although of course in retrospect he was probably like *thirty*, stood up, and said, "We are not here to speak to God. We are here for God to speak to us." Aha, I thought. So I sat there, very patiently, and waited for God to speak to me. I waited and waited and waited, and guess what, He didn't. Or if He did, He certainly didn't introduce himself. So needless to say, after an hour had gone by, I stopped waiting for Him. And eventually I stopped waiting altogether.

EASTER

BY WILL SCHEFFER

WILMA RANSOM — 30s; lovely, enchanting, "special," with an undercurrent of danger and deep sadness. She kind of floats, but is entirely capable of disarming directness and can manipulate shamelessly to get what she wants. She is not crazy, rather she knows something of truth.

SYNOPSIS: It is Good Friday. Matthew and Wilma have set up home in Prattsville, Kansas. Wilma had been burning churches in Oklahoma, forcing the couple to flee across the prairie states. Matthew is hopeful he can make things right for them with a new home and a steady job. Enter Herman, a violin-playing plumber with enormous feet and angel-like qualities, who fixes the couple's sink, only to discover an Easter egg clogging the pipes. Wilma believes the egg is a sign she is pregnant, and thanks Herman by washing his feet with her hair. Meanwhile, the town handyman, Zaddock, has been having religious visions of his own. Upon meeting Matthew, Zaddock recognizes him as one the of the individuals responsible for a church burning in their area. Matthew takes Zaddock hostage and reveals the story of his and Wilma's first baby who died in childbirth and of Wilma's quest for redemption. When Matthew returns home Wilma tries to introduce him to Herman, but Matthew can't see him. Matthew confronts Wilma with her delusion and "shoots" Herman, forcing Wilma to relive the event that caused their estrangement and her intense pain. It is a catharsis long overdue, and Wilma and Matthew must face an uncertain future and begin to rebuild their lives.

WILMA. A baby, Herman! You're doing a beautiful thing. Do you know what it's like to give birth to a baby?
[HERMAN. No.]
WILMA. Oh trust me — it's the most beautiful thing in the

31

world — put your feet up here and I'll tell you about it. A baby being born is like a miracle — but the most beautiful birth in the world, Herman, is when a baby is born feet first.

[HERMAN. *Really?*]

WILMA. Because when a baby comes out feet first, you can see the seven cardinal movements of childbirth. It's the only time you can see them. You can't see them when a baby's born normal, did you know that?

[HERMAN. *No, Wilma, I didn't.*]

WILMA. *(With increasing urgency.)* Well you can't, I studied all about it. But when a baby's born feet first you can see all seven, clear as day. It's special, you see? One: The baby arches his head up and back, to start himself moving down the birth canal and his little feet will come out. Two: He turns to the left to free his right shoulder and Three: to his right to free his left shoulder, and his body appears to spin, just like this, it's spectacular. Four: The baby extends his entire body to prepare to move through the canal and Five: He starts to sort of wiggle as his body pushes it's way out. Six: You see the baby's head coming through the birth opening. This is the most dangerous part of the birth, Herman, because the baby can sometimes suffocate in this position, but Seven: Finally the head will come through and the baby will come out. Because he must come out. Do you understand, Herman? He must come out.

ENGLISH TEACHERS

BY EDWARD NAPIER

POLLY WALKER — 41, English teacher at the sophisticated Huntington High School. Unmarried.

SYNOPSIS: Three generations of women from a respectable family of English teachers live under the same roof in Ceredo, West Virginia, in 1960. Polly, a spinster and grand dame of the Huntington Community Players, brings shame to the family after being fired from teaching for allowing one of her students to read from Allen Ginsberg's epic poem "Howl." This infuriates her widowed sister, Vic, as such a scandal may undermine her effort to be elected as the Democratic candidate for the sixteenth-district seat to the West Virginia House of Delegates. Vic is also concerned about the influence Polly has on her fifteen-year-old daughter, Lib, a baritone-playing misfit of a girl who is madly in love with the handsome boarder, Bobby, a student at nearby Marshall College. Miss Ruthie, Vic's campaign manager, encourages Vic to distance herself from Polly and tries to lure Lib away from Polly's influence by telling Lib she will end up with an unhappy manless life. Mary, the matriarch of the family, tries her best to keep order and peace in her house. In desperation, Polly flees to New York, and, after her brief, failed venture there, turns to Bobby for comfort. Ultimately, Vic wins the election by Miss Ruthie's manipulative shenanigans; Miss Ruthie marries a doctor; Lib becomes a majorette; and Polly ends up working as a check-out clerk.

POLLY.   Well, when I feel like some obscenity — something really twisted and tawdry, I just go straight to the book of Genesis. You know? Where Abraham sold his wife, Sarah — who was also his half-sister, by the way, into prostitution not once but twice: both to Pharaoh and also to King Abimelech of Gerar.

[*MARY. Honey, he had to.*]

POLLY. Yes, I'm sure it was the custom of the time. And then Sarah encouraged her husband-brother Abraham to go in unto her maidservant, Hagar. I mean, it is altogether clear that they were all having quite a raunchy time in the land of Canaan!

[*MARY. Polly, he took her to wife, because Sarah could not conceive.*]

POLLY. Of course, my favorite sordid section of the book of Genesis, however, is where Lot's daughters get their father drunk and seduce him right after the destruction of Sodom and Gomorrah. I mean — *(Laughs.)*

[*RUTHIE. Is she committing blasphemy?*]

POLLY. *[No, Darling Ruth,]* I'm simply retelling stories from the Holy Scriptures, yours and mine. Read them. They're shocking. But then, so is Mr. Ginsberg, of course, as most good literature is. But his line you keep referring to Ruthie, "The tongue, the cock, the hand, the asshole holy" endeavors to convey the fact that all aspects of existence, experience are holy — indeed, divine. It could be argued that, to a degree, "Footnote to Howl" is inspired by and is almost a literary reference to Psalm 139, God where shall I go, to heaven or hell, but there you are. Holy God. Holy cock, asshole, and to remain within the spirit of the poem, one would say, cunt, I suppose …

EPIC PROPORTIONS

BY LARRY COEN AND DAVID CRANE

LOUISE GOLDMAN — 20s–30s, an attractive young woman.

SYNOPSIS: Set in the 1930s, this play tells the story of two brothers, Benny and Phil, who go to the Arizona desert to be extras in the huge Biblical epic film Exeunt Omnes. *Things more very quickly in this riotous comedy and before you know it, Phil is directing the movie and Benny is starring in it. To complicate matters further, they both fall in love with Louise, the Assistant Director in charge of the extras, and now playing an Egyptian princess.*

LOUISE. *(She enters, carrying a clipboard.)* Okay. How 'bout that, huh? And you guys: not bad for a first time, or "first take" as you'll hear it called. For those of you who came in on the buses last night and don't know me, my name is Louise Goldman and I'm the Assistant Director in charge of Atmosphere Personnel, or "Extras." That's you. Now there are more than 3,400 of you out there, so it may take me a little while to get to know all your names. But I want you to know that if you have any problems, you can always come to me. I'm in the little blue tent next to the Sphinx of Antioch, and my flap is always open. So welcome to Molten Rock, Arizona, where we will be filming the D.W. Dewitt production of *Exeunt Omnes*, which apparently is Latin for "everybody out." Who knew? I think you'll be excited to know that you are going to be part of the biggest epic ever made. If you look around, you can see that construction has already begun on over five hundred sets recreating the Ancient World from the Old Testament to Empire to the Land of the Pharaohs. *(She consults h*
Now, even though the nearest town is over 240 miles
scorching desert, that doesn't mean we can't have fun ri

I've got a sign-up sheet for softball that I'll be posting by the Temple of Osiris, on the bulletin board next to the Oracle. Oh, and if anyone has a softball, that'd be great. Okay, I realize many of you have never acted in a motion picture before. Well, let me just say that if we all work together, then we'll have something we can all really be proud of. And I'm sorry there are only two bathrooms. All right, we're going to divide you up into a few groups for different scenes. So would you please count off by four, starting here.

THE EROS TRILOGY

BY NICKY SILVER

CLAIRE — a beautiful woman, past 40, who possesses the grace and delicacy of another era.

SYNOPSIS: THE EROS TRILOGY is a collection of three short, thematically related pieces, CLAIRE, PHILIP and ROGER & MIRIAM. CLAIRE, the first piece, finds a beautiful matron who might have walked out of a Noel Coward play. Claire is trying to recover from an incident that occurred in the morning, an incident which brought home, all too painfully, the reality that the beautiful world which she called home is gone forever. Shaken and frightened, she finds peace only while making love with a much younger man, a man who allows her to forget herself and retreat into a world where "we were children and easily pleased."

CLAIRE Children are an odd phenomenon, don't you find? I have to say, I've never really understood them. It seems so irrational to me. You create something. You carry something around, inside of you, for what seems an eternity, and then you are delivered a person. A stranger. And you can tell me otherwise, but from the minute we're born, we are people. My children had likes and dislikes from day one. Philip, like me, adored beauty and music. He longed to compose before he could read. While Amy, on the other hand, turned her nose up at my breast and never really came around!

(Lecturing.) I see young mothers in the park walking their children, like poodles on leashes. I am aghast! They treat their children as if they were objects. I claim no expertise *BUT* it has been my experience that children are not dogs. Were they dogs, I'm afraid, I'd've been tempted to put Amy to sleep several times by

now. I don't mean to be hard about Amy. I'm sure she has many fine qualities — which are not apparent to me. All people have goodness inside of them! Only some people have very little, and it's *very, very, very* deep down. And she is a stranger! That's what it comes down to. I know she came from me, but she's not part of — oh, God. I must sound awful. But it's true. My feet are part of me. My hands are part of me. My children are people I know. I do love them. Don't mistake my objectivity for indifference. I love my children very much. I just see that they are *other* people. And, if you ask me, we'd have a great deal less crime and drug addiction if mothers and fathers realized their children are not their pets. And this understanding would lead to happier children, healthier adults, less crime, lower taxes, a thriving economy, prettier architecture, less television, more theater, less litigation, more understanding, less alienation, more love, less hate and a calmer humanity who felt less of a need to spit all the time in public!!

EVERY SEVENTEEN MINUTES THE CROWD GOES CRAZY!

BY PAUL ZINDEL

MAUREEN — one of the older kids, wants to be a magazine writer; she's gorgeous to watch because of her hair and that she is a thing in motion at all times. She's lost in her own articulateness and she's terribly cunning with her beauty; she runs around the apartment houses making believe she's collecting for Catholic Charities whenever she needs money to treat her boyfriends for a date. She's hot as a pistol. She's a young Marilyn Monroe on speed and with a high IQ — tarot cards, other-world experiences, waiting to be abducted by aliens.

SYNOPSIS: A family of exuberant and startled kids are left to fend for themselves by their mother and father — who have taken off to pursue forever a life of betting at trotter racetracks and playing black-jack in Native American casinos! An expandable chorus punctuates with hilarious and stinging sound bites this highly theatrical and poignant legend of parental abdication.

MAUREEN. I see ... a carnival. That's what I see.
[...]
It starts pretty ... lights, and rides, cotton candy and a kind of tinkling music ...
[...]
... it looks beautiful at first ... but then something happens ...
[...]
I mean, there are lights and rides ... but the merry-go-r

turning backwards ... When I look close at everything, it's all spinning, turning backwards. That's when I start to get frightened. I see trees, mangrove trees — and their roots are growing upwards. And there are fish. Strange glistening fish that can climb the trees. And then suddenly, I realize the carnival is in a swamp. A swamp where a tiger is loose. A tiger that's after me ... it's after everyone. It's like tigers I read about in a Bengal swamp — where they have to drink salt water and it changes their brains ... and when I look at the people in the swamp carnival, I see they're all frightened, too. They have babies on their shoulders, and they're holding balloons, and everyone knows the tiger is after them. It's a tiger that won't attack you if you're looking at it — and so I start to run, I run spinning, trying to look everywhere so the tiger won't get me. And I see the people are all wearing masks on the back of their heads — masks with big smiles and eyes painted on them, masks to fool the tiger — they hope the tiger won't know it's a mask — but the tiger's on to their trick. I want to cry out, "The masks don't work anymore! They don't work!" but the sounds get caught in my throat and they sound like ...
[...]
I don't know. I don't know.

AN EXPERIMENT WITH AN AIR PUMP

BY SHELAGH STEPHENSON

MARIA — a young Englishwoman in 1799.

SYNOPSIS: The play takes place in a home in Northern England in 1799 and the present day — eras on the thresholds of new centuries and new worlds. In 1799 the Fenwick household awaits a future in which Dr. Fenwick believes science will bring about an enlightened democratic society. But Fenwick is blind to the ignorance and inequalities right under his nose. His protege, Armstrong, recklessly toys with the affections of Isobel, the crippled servant girl, and his daughter Maria pines after her faithless fiancé in India. Meanwhile, in the present day, all of the scientific advancements of the past 200 years have produced more questions. Ellen is a geneticist, who inherited the house from her mother. The upkeep for the old house is expensive, and she and her husband, Tom, may have to sell it. Ellen has been offered a good job, which might mean they could keep the house, but Tom has ethical problems with the job because it involves fetal tissue research. And into this mix comes the mystery of the skeleton of a long-dead girl found buried under the kitchen floor.

MARIA. Dear Edward,
You are right, England is cold and bleak, and so, I might add is my heart. Either distance has dimmed your perception of me, or you never looked properly at me from the start. Imagine my eyes again, Edward. Now write and tell me what colour they appear in your imagination. Your early letters were so full of longing for me and for home, but now I sense a reluctance to return which cannot entirely be explained by the prevailing weather conditions. I

41

hear, via a Mr. Roger Thornton, who has recently returned from Lucknow, that a certain Miss Cholmondely has stayed in India rather longer than expected. Could this be the same musical creature you mention in your letters? She who sinks into a dead faint when confronted by native antiquities? Her eyes, I gather, are a quite startling blue. I note that when you think of England now you remember dead boys frozen in the top meadow. Hitherto you imagined soft sunlight and balmy breezes and gentle Englishmen full of decorum and equanimity. I now realise that your vision of England was as flawed as your recollection of my eyes. Yes, it is true that here we may freeze to death in winter. Indeed our summers are mild. But temperate we are not. Need I remind you that we have had bloody riots here for at least six months, and that my father, the finest Englishman I know, has never been anything less than passionate. As you know, Edward, I have long been regarded as the mild, perhaps even silly half of the heavenly twins, very much in Harriet's poetic shadow. That, presumably, is what attracted you to me in the first place. (But Miss Cholmondely is clearly the better swooner.) I find now however, that anger has provoked my intellect like a spark igniting a long dormant volcano. I await your reply with interest.

Sincerely, Maria Fenwick.

FROM ABOVE

BY TOM DONAGHY

EVVY — a woman in her 40s.

SYNOPSIS: Evvy, in her 40s, was married to Jimmy, in his 70s. She has been in mourning a year since he died and now her friends want her seclusion to end. Sean, a local social worker, has been trying to woo her, to no avail. Evvy's neighbor, Linny, seems to have a crush on her. What shocks Evvy out of mourning is the arrival of Jimmy, an attractive young man who says he's her late husband. He knows details about their house, her favorite foods, even where he stores his pipe tobacco. Unnerved by this, Evvy gives way to the stranger even though he's clearly disoriented and possibly dangerous. But the chance to spend time with her husband again is too good to pass up, even if it is only make-believe. When Evvy's friends show up, Jimmy flees and isn't heard from again until months later. Upon his return, he tells Evvy he's come from the local mental hospital and that her late husband was an old and trusted coworker. With the mystery solved, Jimmy leaves, and Evvy looks at Sean and resolves to experience, at close range, what might be next.

EVVY.   He never took anything! *(Beat.)* I dream, I daydream and I think, he never took anything. And then I come out of it. But then I'm at work, doing something, preparing something or other and I'm sane and I'm thinking, what if things happened — and I'm not missing anything from the house —
[LINNY.   Sweetie.]
EVVY.   Well, my watch I'm missing, but I gave that to him and I never liked knowing time anyway — but what if things happened, I think? If things came back to you in ways you couldn't — and I'm not crazy — but events, you know? And then I wake up.

I was almost fired, you know, in the laundry room. I'd stopped folding sheets. I was thinking, I was sitting in a pile of sheets, thinking, everything unfolded and we were expecting that convention and someone from housekeeping rushed in and said "What are you doing? We need these sheets!" And I said, "This room is soft." Then you come out of it. You make sense of things. You walk home. You piece together some sense. It's some boy near Linny's sister's. Or to steal things. And I come home and I see something move in the grass but so fast and I think — I think — *(Beat.)* I wanted to be an altar boy. We weren't Catholic. I was tiny and you believe things. God could make things happen, I thought. I was tiny, but, but — nothing happens here, we get on each other's nerves, you know nothing happens here, we have crushes on each other, it's the same and the same maybe — and maybe once —

[LINNY. *I didn't know.*]

EVVY.   — And he never took anything.

[LINNY. *Sweetie.*]

EVVY.   Maybe once something happened.

FUDDY MEERS

BY DAVID LINDSAY-ABAIRE

CLAIRE — about 40, a generally sunny woman with amnesia.

SYNOPSIS: Claire has a rare form of psychogenic amnesia that erases her memory whenever she goes to sleep. This morning, like all mornings, she wakes up a blank slate. Her chipper husband comes in with a cup of coffee, explains her condition, hands her a book filled with all sorts of essential information, and he disappears into the shower. A limping, lisping, half-blind, half-deaf man in a ski mask pops out from under her bed and claims to be her brother, there to save her. Claire's info book is quickly discarded, and she's hustled off to the country house of her mother, Gertie, a recent stroke victim whose speech has been reduced to utter gibberish. Claire's journey gets even more complicated when a dimwitted thug with a foul-mouthed hand puppet pops up at a window, and her driven husband and perpetually stoned son show up with a claustrophobic lady-cop that they've kidnapped. Every twist and turn in this fun-house plot brings Claire closer to revealing her past life and everything she thought she'd forgotten. It's one harrowing and hilarious turn after another on this roller coaster ride through the day of an amnesiac trying to decipher her fractured life.

CLAIRE.   […] You remember that dog? Skinny old thing Mr. Cuthart kept tied up in the front lawn all day? Daddy always said he was gonna report him. Remember she just sat in the sun, biting at her scabs? Cuthart didn't even give her any water.
[GERTIE.   *Who do teching bat?*]
CLAIRE.   [*Nancy.*] So I'd sneak down the road with my squirt gun, and spritz water into her mouth and she'd bark.
[GERTIE.   *Uh-huh. I bee rye bag. (Rushes off to another part of the house.)*]

CLAIRE.   And one day, when Cuthart was downtown, I untied her to let her run around a little. But she darted straight into the road, just as Daddy's pickup was coming around the curve, and he didn't see her, so he plowed into her. Do you remember Daddy and I came through the back door, Mama? And Nancy was hanging out of his arms like a set of broken-up bagpipes. And he spread her out on the kitchen floor and she was breathing real hard. And the pain was humming off of her like I could hear it. And she just let the pain take her over. And that's all she was. This *pained* thing. And Daddy was bent over her, talking to her real quiet. And all of sudden Nancy stood up, like it was a new day, and she started running around the kitchen like she wasn't half-dead, barking and clicking her nails against the floor tiles. And we were all shocked because Nancy was like a puppy all of a sudden, not that bony heap on the floor. She was this fireball for about three minutes, until she got tired again, and curled up beside the sink and went to sleep and died like it meant nothing. You remember how all that happened in here? It's funny how almost everything else is gone to me, and that sad old dog just came into my head.

GIVE ME YOUR ANSWER, DO!

BY BRIAN FRIEL

DAISY CONNOLLY — Bridget's mother, in her early 40. She pays little attention to her appearance. Her hair, clothes, body are not neglected, just forgotten about.

SYNOPSIS: The play is set in the home of the impoverished Irish novelist, Tom Connolly, and his wife, Daisy, whose lives are overshadowed by Bridget, their permanently hospitalized daughter. They are visited by Daisy's parents and by the successful novelist, Garret Fitzgerald, and his wife, Gráinne. The question at the heart of the play is: Will Connolly sell his manuscripts to a Texas university (as Fitzgerald has just done) and thus acquire some much-needed money? This is a story of people inextricably bound together and of the loves and hates that that proximity generates.

DAISY. Oh, no, he mustn't sell. Of course he mustn't sell. There are reasons why he wants to sell and those reasons are valid reasons and understandable and very persuasive. A better place for Bridget. Escape from the tyranny of those daily bills and the quick liberation that would offer. Maybe a house with just a little comfort. And if David's offer is as large as he suggests, then of course the most persuasive reason of all: The work has value — yes, yes, yes! Here is the substantial confirmation, the tangible evidence! The work *must* be good! I'm not imprisoned in the dark anymore! Now I can run again! Now I can *dare* again! *(Pause.)*
    Yes, it is so very persuasive. I convinced myself I believed in all those arguments, too — I think because I knew they were so attractive, almost irresistible, to him. But we were both deluded. Indeed

we were. A better place for Bridget? But Bridget is beyond knowing, isn't she? And somehow, somehow bills will always be met. And what does a little physical discomfort matter? Really not a lot. But to sell for an affirmation, for an answer, to be free of that grinding uncertainty, that would be so wrong for him and so wrong for his work. Because that uncertainty is necessary. He must live with that uncertainty, that necessary uncertainty. Because there can be no verdicts, no answers. Indeed there *must* be no verdicts. Because being alive is the postponement of verdicts, isn't it? Because verdicts are provided only when it's all over, all concluded.

Of course he mustn't sell.

And now I'm going to pour myself a little gin. And only half an hour ago I made a secret vow to give up gin forever and ever and to switch to health-giving red wine. But there you are — the road to hell — touch of a slut — and so we stagger on — To the Necessary Uncertainty.

GOOD AS NEW

BY PETER HEDGES

MAGGIE — a girl of 16.

SYNOPSIS: A brutal comedy on the secrets people keep, GOOD AS NEW follows the disintegration of an educated, affluent Chicago family — parents, Dennis and Jan, and teenage daughter, Maggie — following Mom's face-lift. Devastated by what she views as a violation of who her mother is — an enlightened feminist — the daughter confronts Mom. Mom in turn blurts out that she took the nip-and-tuck route because she's losing Dad and suspects he is having an affair. Further shattered, the girl now engages in a face-off with her father, who defends himself by saying Mom has also "wandered." The first act begins with Maggie driving her father to the airport.

MAGGIE. Nervous?
[DENNIS. No. (Beat.)]
MAGGIE. Did you know that while teenagers make up only five percent of the driving population, they are responsible for thirty-five percent of all traffic accidents? Did you know that in the state of Illinois, three out of five traffic fatalities are caused by drivers under the age of twenty-five? And you say you're not nervous?
[DENNIS. That's right.]
MAGGIE. Well, you should be.
[DENNIS. Not about this.]
MAGGIE. Oh, like you, I resisted some of these statistics. I thought, no way, not possible. Did you know three out of every four accidents happen within a mile of the driver's residence? Well, think about it: Around your home you tend to relax, you ease up, you've done the same turn a thousand times — that's wh
have to be extra careful. This is why, I suppose, they drille

49

the five Fundamentals of Driver's Ed. These helpful hints are supposed to keep us alert. Like: Get the Big Picture. That's when you see the whole situation. See who's behind you, what's up ahead, what your options are, how to best keep your distance. There are other slogans: Keep Your Eyes Moving. Check Your Blind Spot. Leave Yourself an Out. Make Sure Others See You. Do these things and the promise is maybe you won't crash! *(Beat.)* Admit you're nervous.

[DENNIS. Maggie, you're a very good driver.]

MAGGIE. I better be good. Months of classes, video simulation, weekly drives with Mr. Moore who is very serious about all this ... it's his church! Mr. Moore, every day a new slogan on the chalkboard: Treat every child like a walking caution sign. If you love your children, belt them! But what gets me ... there's a girl in my class — Becky Chandler — six months pregnant. She's going to keep the child, a lot of people think "How great." The saddest truth? She's already had more training to be a driver than she'll ever get to be a parent — it makes me wonder about our priorities, as a people. And, also, you know what? Becky Chandler, who got her driving certificate the same day I did, *can't even parallel park!*

THE HOLOGRAM THEORY

BY JESSICA GOLDBERG

RITAH LEVINO — 25, Brooklyn-Italian. She is the fiancée of
the police officer Patsy goes to for help.

*SYNOPSIS: A beautiful, young Trinidadian artist, Patsy, is awak-
ened one night to a vision of her twin brother, Dominic, whom she
hasn't seen in five years. Unbeknownst to Patsy, he has been mur-
dered, and his restless ghost summons her to unravel the mystery of
his death and what was once his life. Patsy travels to the decadent,
seductive and terrifying underworld of New York City and finds
herself in a foreign world — a vast landscape of club kids, cops and
jaded journalists. As she learns more about the brutal world her
brother once inhabited, as well his own brutality, Patsy struggles
with complex feelings about her past, familial obligations and the
spirit world.*

RITAH. Mah? Hi, how are you? I'm fine. Looking through
Bridal Guide. God I just love the Tiffany china. Sucks I couldn't
register there, but all my friends would be able to afford would
be the paperweights. Yeah, he called. He had to work overtime
or somethin' tonight. I hate when he works at night. I get
scared. I should sleep at your house these nights, least that way
I could get some rest. All's I do is keep lookin' at the clock. I'm
sure I wanna marry him, c'mon. Just he told me this story, 'bout
this head and, oh never mind. Just lonely, and nervous. The
head, there was a head in the morgue disappeared. I know I
asked for it, marrying a cop. It's just I got this funny feeling, like
what if Greg has the head? Ughh, sorry. Sorry. I'm bein' so stu-

pid. Maybe I should start workin' that feminine charm I inherited from you, get him to quit. I could do that. Right? Okay, yeah, no it's fine I understand, you got to put Dad to bed. I'm sorry. I love ya, Mah.

HONOUR

BY JOANNA MURRAY-SMITH

SOPHIE — 24-year-old daughter of Gus and Honor.

SYNOPSIS: After thirty-two years, a marriage shatters into pieces. Acclaimed journalist Gus leaves Honor, a poet, wife and mother, for Claudia, a bright young journalist not much older than his and Honor's twenty-four-year-old daughter, Sophie. In the wake of new passion stands Honor, who must come to grips with the career she has willingly sacrificed for her husband and child, the evolution of a marriage, her abandonment and eventual resurrection. Gus must face the consequences of betraying his own long-held principles about duty and justice, of leaving a secure love for the raptures of passion. Claudia confronts the darkness of her own impulses and learns that to love truly and wisely is to understand moral responsibility. In a series of intense confrontations, the wife, husband, lover and daughter negotiate the forces of passion, lust, history, responsibility and honour.

[CLAUDIA. *You think I bewitched your father? (Beat.) He loves me. (Beat.)*]
SOPHIE. Well, I suppose he might. *(Pause.)* I wish — I wish I was more — *(Beat.)* Like you. Like you. You're so — you're so clear. You seem so clear about things. Whereas I'm — I'm so — I can never quite say what I'm — even to myself, I'm so inarticulate. *(Beat.)* Some nights I lie awake and I go over the things I've said. Confidently. The things I've said confidently and they — they fall to pieces. *(Beat.)* And where there were words there is now just — just this feeling of — of *impossibility.* That everything is — there's no way through it — *(Beat. Progressively breaking down.)* I used to feel that way when I was very small. That same feeling. Not a

53

childish feeling — well, maybe. As if I was choking on — as if life was coming down on me and I couldn't see my way through it. What does a child who has everything suffer from? Who could name it? I can't. I can't. *(Breaking.)* But it was a — a sort of — I used to see it in my head as jungle. Around me. Surrounding me. Some darkness growing, something — organic, alive — and the only thing that kept me — kept me — *here* — was the picture of Honor and of Gus. Silly. *(Beat.)* Because I'm old now and I shouldn't remember that anymore. Lying in bed and feeling that they were there: outside the room in all their — their warmth, their — a kind of charm to them. Maybe you're right and it was — not so simple as it looked, but they gave such a strong sense of — love for each other and inside that — *I* felt — *I* felt loved. And since I've gotten older I don't feel — *(Weeping.)* I feel as if all that — all the — everything that saved me has fallen from me and you know, I'm not a kid anymore. No. I'm not a kid anymore. But I still feel — I need — I need — *(Pause. Collecting herself.)* Sorry.

IMPOSSIBLE MARRIAGE

BY BETH HENLEY

FLORAL WHITMAN — 30, older sister of the bride.

SYNOPSIS: The entire action of the play takes place in Kandall Kingsley's beautiful and mysterious garden. Kandall's youngest daughter, Pandora, is to be wed to Edvard Lunt, a worldly artist twice her age. Kandall does not think the match to be at all suitable. Floral, Pandora's older sister, who is expecting a child at any moment, plots to break off the marriage. Unexpectedly, Sidney Lunt, the groom's son, arrives with a note from his mother in which she vows to throw herself from an attic window if the marriage goes forward. Even Reverend Lawrence, who has come to wed the couple, has secret hopes and desperate desires.

FLORAL. Last night there was a little misunderstanding between us that I must rectify. When I said there could be a circus performing under my skirt, I was implying — it was meant to be a joke. I was attempting to indicate, I was wearing a tent, a large, billowy dress. Because of the pregnancy I was so big and wearing such large garb, i.e., tents, that a circus could or would be capable of performing underneath. You (I assume) assumed I meant I could service a whole circus, I mean an entire company of clowns or whatever could come under my skirt with their lascivious little ladders and horns and party, party, party or whatever. Actually, it was a joke I could have phrased more carefully. Still your interpretation was not warranted.
[EDVARD. In attempting to follow your amorphous train of thought, I seem to have derailed.]
FLORAL. In any case, I'd like you to know I'm extraordinarily particular about who I see privately. I'm not a virgin, but other than that, I am wholesome in the extreme. Having said that, I beg you to leave.

55

IN THE BLOOD

BY SUZAN-LORI PARKS

AMIGA GRINGA — Hester's friend.

SYNOPSIS: A modern day riff on The Scarlet Letter, *Hester La Negrita, a homeless mother of five, lives with her kids on the tough streets of the inner city. Her eldest child is teaching her how to read and write, but so far the letter "A" is the only letter she knows. Her five kids are named Jabber, Bully, Trouble, Beauty and Baby, and the characters are played by adult actors who double as five other people in Hester's life: her ex-boyfriend, her social worker, her doctor, her best friend and her minister. While Hester's kids fill her life with joy the adults with whom she comes in contact only hold her back. Nothing can stop the play's tragic end.*

AMIGA GRINGA.
In my head I got it going on.
The triple X rated movie:
Hester and Amiga get down and get dirty.
Chocolate and Vanilla get into the ugly.
We coulda done a sex show behind a curtain
Then make a movie and sell it
for 3 bucks a peek.
I had me some delicious schemes
to get her out of that hole she calls home.
Im doing well for myself
working my money maker
Do you have any idea how much cash I'll get for the fruit of my
    white womb?!
Grow it.
Birth it.

Sell it.
And why shouldnt I?
(Rest.)
Funny how a woman like Hester
driving her life all over the road
most often chooses to walk the straight and narrow.
Girl on girl action is a very lucrative business.
And someones gotta do something for her.
Im just trying to help her out.
And myself too, ok. They dont call it Capitalizm for nothing.
(Rest.)
She liked the idea of the sex
at least she acted like it.
Her looking at me with those eyes of hers
You looking like you want it, Hester
Shoot, Miga, she says thats just the way I look she says.
It took a little cajoling to get her to do it with me
For an invited audience.
For a dime a look.
Over at my place.
Every cent was profit and no overhead to speak of.
The guys in the neighborhood got their pleasure
and we was our own boss so we didnt have to pay no joker off the top.
We slipped right into a very profitable situation
like sliding into warm water.
Her breasts her bottom
She let me touch her however I wanted
I let her ride my knees
She made sounds like an animal.
She put her hand between my legs.
One day some of the guys took advantage.
Ah, what do you expect in a society based on Capitalizm.
I tell you the plight of the worker these days — .
Still one day Im gonna get her to make the movie
Cause her and me we had the moves down
very sensual, very provocative, very scientific, very lucrative.
In my head I got it going on.

THE JOY OF GOING SOMEWHERE DEFINITE

BY QUINCY LONG

MARIE — an attractive young woman with spiritual aspirations.

SYNOPSIS: Three out-of-work loggers, fueled by alcohol, God and song, set forth from a northwoods bar one night on a misguided errand of mercy. Raymond, Merle and Junior have met a stranger in the bar even drunker and lonelier than they are, and, after accidentally shooting him, decide to reunite him with his estranged wife, Marie, at a religious community somewhere north of the border in Canada. Hampered at every turn by misunderstanding, confusion, stupidity, drunkenness, desire and mistaken identity, the chivalrous loggers resolutely attempt to do the right thing, while achieving precisely the opposite. In the end, wild certainty yields to a chastened amazement over what man won't do for a little peace.

MARIE.
    I mean we weren't on the lake
    Actually on the lake
    But you could see the water
[...]
    And my parents they had this old four poster you had to
            climb this little steps up to get up on the mattress
    Had a canopy over top of it
[...]
    We'd imagine we were in some old period
    Romantic or
    I would anyways
    I don't know what was in his mind about it

58

He

He

He just liked it I guess

And I liked that he liked it

But then he got sent away for robbing and

I mean it really messed me up

The trauma of all that

And that was it

The beginning of me being into the behavior problems of a
teenager in her teens doing a lot of stuff with a lot of
people I wasn't supposed to 'til he

[...]

Well anyway he's in the Navy now and he was

Oh he was mad

So mad at me for the way I am now 'cause he says he loves
me and

We're married see now but

But he gets so kind of psycho all the time that

To the point he threatens to kill me and I just

I take out a court order but he's so

He doesn't care about that and it ends up I just came away
from the lake and even that doesn't stop me from my
problems

It's actually worse now like I'm on this pattern I can't control
to get myself all

Messed up

And it

It leads to death

I know that

I know it

Total death this

Total

But God see

God

God

I know that He doesn't see me like this

I know it

Like I see it

My
Me
God He's just the most important thing for me
My core
The whole core of my whole behavior that I never really had
And everything else
It's just out of my
Out of my hands
That whole other way of life
That's over now
Completely over for me
And I
I mean I think about it sometimes
In the distance I mean
What he's
Claude's
Claude
But that's
Anyway I just got this prayer that goes over and over from so
        deep inside that I can
We can be healed from our past and
It
I just need a peace and quiet and a a a a
A study of it you know to
Of the whole way it
A study of the things of the spirit and how it fits together
        with these things in my life because
[…]
I've done stupid things in my
With my life but I
[…]
No.

LAKE HOLLYWOOD

BY JOHN GUARE

AGNES — late 30s, at the start of the play, to late 70s.

SYNOPSIS: Act One finds us at Scroon Lake, New Hampshire in August 1940. Agnes and Andrew arrive at Agnes' home, which she shares with her sister, Flo, who would like to have the home all for herself. Also at the lake are Flo's oddly infantile husband, Randolph, and Randolph's mother, Mrs. Larry, who speaks with a false German accent. The woods around the lake are ablaze, threatening the house, and many of their belongings have been brought down to the beach, including Agnes' beloved credenza, which has been in the family for years. Agnes' Uncle Ambrose appears and shares his tale of Spencer Tracy's visit to Scroon Lake and his dream of turning the lake into Lake Hollywood, a retreat for Hollywood stars. The second act leaps forward forty years and to New York City. Agnes and Andrew, now husband and wife, are preparing to take Agnes to the hospital where she must undergo an operation. Hildegarde, their daughter, along with her husband and child, arrives to take them to the hospital, but Andrew and Agnes escape the apartment and take a walk. Along the way, they stop at a restaurant where their waiter turns out to be a young man Agnes knew when he was a child. He is kind to them, and Agnes decides to leave the credenza to him, since no one in the family wants it. As they continue on to the hospital, we are left with the image of two people living their lives not with Hollywood magic but with the reality of their love and friendship as a couple.

AGNES. *(In a breath.)* Me! Me! Me! When I was fifteen, I had a job at McGrath's in Alton Bay helping at the soda fountain and one day after work I walked back home. It was August the fifteenth. I had my bathing suit on under my uniform. I wanted to get in the water because of the cure. I heard a car behind me which was a rare sight on the lake road. I stopped to let it pass. The snazzy convertible stops and this guy opens the door, "Get in. You want a ride?" I never been in a snazzy car. We drove off. Red leather seats. I loved being in that car. I put my legs up on the dashboard. I told him all about the Blessed Mother and the cure in the water. He leaned close. He said I was very interesting. I thanked him. He put his hand on my leg. His hand was very cool. I could see the lake. He pulled off the main road onto the grass. He put his hand up under my uniform and got hold of the strap on my bathing suit. I said this is not the way to the lake. He ripped the strap on my bathing suit and put his face close to me. He stuck out his tongue. It had a white peppermint drop on it. He reached to kiss me. I bit into his face. I flew out of the car. I ran like a deer. I could hear his footsteps behind me. I was at the water's edge. I could taste his blood on my mouth where I bit him. I jumped in the lake and started swimming. He ran along the shore holding his face, yelling, "I'll get you. Wherever you go, I'll get you. You led me on. You led me on." I swam and swam until I saw home and Flo standing by the cabin door, holding a yellow piece of paper which was a telegram from Boston saying our parents had both died of the Spanish flu. "You led me on." I never told anybody what happened. My sister Flo or Uncle Ambrose or anybody. I'd lay awake for nights, waiting for him to get me. "You led me on." I came to New York to get away. I married you, but he was always there, looking for me. "You led me on." I was always afraid I'd do something famous like be the millionth person to ride on the subway and my name would get in the paper and he'd see it and come get me. "You led me on." All these years I lay low. I never turned him in. I never mentioned him. *(Pause.)* And now I have.

THE LARAMIE PROJECT

BY MOISÉS KAUFMAN AND THE MEMBERS OF
THE TECTONIC THEATER PROJECT

REGGIE FLUTY — a policewoman. 30s/40s.

SYNOPSIS: In October 1998 a twenty-one-year-old student at the University of Wyoming was severely beaten and left to die, tied to a fence in the middle of the prairie outside Laramie. His bloody, bruised and battered body was not discovered until the next day, and he died in an area hospital several days later. His name was Matthew Shepard, and he was the victim of this assault because he was gay. Moisés Kaufman and members of the Tectonic Theater Project made six trips to Laramie over a year and a half in the aftermath of the beating and during the trial. They conducted over 200 interviews with people from the town and constructed a theatrical collage, exploring the depths to which humanity can sink and the heights of compassion we are also capable of.

REGGIE FLUTY: I responded to the call.
[…]
When I got there, the first — at first the only thing I could see was partially somebody's feet and I got out of my vehicle and raced over — I seen what appeared to be a young man, thirteen, fourteen years old because he was so tiny laying on his back and he was tied to the bottom end of a pole.

I did the best I could. The gentleman that was laying on the ground, Matthew Shepard, he was covered in dry blood all over his head. There was dry blood underneath him and he was barely breathing … he was doing the best he could.

I was going to breathe for him and I couldn't get his mouth open — his mouth wouldn't open for me.

He was covered in, like I said, partially dry blood and blood all over his head — the only place that he did not have any blood on him, on his face, was what appeared to be where he had been crying down his face.

His head was distorted. You know, it did not look normal — he looked as if he had a real harsh head wound.

[...]

He was tied to the fence — his hands were thumbs out in what we call a cuffing position — the way we handcuff people. He was bound with a real thin white rope. It went around the bottom of the pole, about four inches up off the ground.

His shoes were missing.

He was tied extremely tight — so I used my boot knife and tried to slip it between the rope and his wrist — I had to be extremely careful not to harm Matthew any further.

[...]

He was bound so tight — I finally got the knife through there — I'm sorry — we rolled him over to his left side — when we did that he quit breathing. Immediately, I put him back on his back — and that was just enough of an adjustment — it gave me enough room to cut him free there.

I seen the EMS unit trying to get to the location. Once the ambulance got there we put a neck collar on him, placed him on a back board and scooted him from underneath the fence — then Rob drove the ambulance to Ivanson Hospital's Emergency Room ...

[...]

They showed me a picture ... days later I saw a picture of Matthew ... I would have never recognized him.

LOVE AND UNDERSTANDING

BY JOE PENHALL

RACHEL — late 20s or 30s.

SYNOPSIS: Live-in lovers Neal and Rachel are overworked doctors. They rarely see each other and their relationship suffers for it. Enter Neal's old good-for-nothing friend, Richie, for a surprise visit. He needs a place to stay and Neal is too weak to say no. Rachel doesn't want him either, but Richie manipulates her, creating a sexual tension between them. Richie immediately uses this charge to stir up trouble between the couple, insinuating that Neal is boring and that Rachel needs a good time with a black sheep like himself. And while he works on Rachel, Richie steals drugs from Neal's office. Rachel tells Neal about the pass, but Richie denies it. Thinking Neal doesn't care, Rachel sleeps with Richie, but the couple is caught by Neal. Richie almost delights in the trouble he's caused, and with more drugs, ends up comatose from an overdose. The strain of all that's happened causes Rachel and Neal to split up. Richie recovers, and takes off for Wales, leaving Neal and Rachel with a new-found understanding of one another which may or may not lead to reconciliation.

RACHEL.   Oh I've had enough of this. *(She starts to go.)*
[NEAL.   *Don't walk away from me when I'm talking to you.]*
RACHEL.   I thought we could do this together. I thought you might like to help me. I thought if we did this together and we talked about it and we ... talked about a few other things it might be a bit easier. I thought I could come over and we could go through our things and talk about it properly and separate our things and then when this is all over ... when I find somewhere to

go ... you could come over for dinner or something. I thought I'd cook you dinner. I thought it would be nice. I thought I was making a gesture. I thought it might help me to say I'm sorry. Because I am sorry. I am ... so sorry, Neal ... and I'm trying not to make a scene and I'm trying to be sensitive about this and I'm trying ... not to be so sensitive about this and just get on with it ... I'm trying to be practical ... I'm trying not to get all emotional about it ... that's why I took the stupid fucking wok.

MARCUS IS WALKING

BY JOAN ACKERMANN

CAITLIN — a librarian, an intellectual, her clothes a little disheveled, artsy, wears glasses; not at all fashion-conscious. She is charming in an offhanded, Annie Hall kind of way.

SYNOPSIS: Eleven vignettes in an automobile examine the emotional landscape we roam as we travel in our cars. Control, navigation, love and escape are some of the themes explored. A protective father shepherds his son through the neighborhood on Halloween; an actor on his way to perform Hamlet provokes a rear-end collision and confrontation with a Czech émigré cab driver; a devastated businessman strikes up an unlikely alliance with a homeless woman who sleeps in his car. This is the landscape of human frailty and vulnerability, charm and strength; a playwright's whimsy combined with a shrewd sense of observation.

CAITLIN. *(Chattily, merrily, thoroughly enjoying herself.)* I'm not going to do just fine, I tell you that right now. I'm going to freak out. I haven't been back here in two years. Not since it happened. Now it takes me six hours to drive to Boston on back roads instead of two and a half. Did you know that one out of eight women have panic attacks? One out of eight. That's a lot of panic. I know it's psychological at this point. I know it's all in my head but I can't control it, ooo could you take your hand off my thigh please? I like your hand, it's just a little distracting. It's like the road freezes in a freeze frame, things stop moving as a video, and my mind jams into this ... ozone ... *warp* and it's *exhausting* like I'm towing the car with my brain and I can't breathe and I get disconnected from my body and I think I'll pass out. I never *have* passed out but I think I will. If there's a breakdown lane, it doesn't happen; if there isn't one, it's … God, it's indescribably awful. Zack, could you please stop chewing on my ear; it's kind of noisy. Maybe you'd like to come by later. *(She can't believe her audacity.)* The weird thing, I'm more afraid of the fear than I am of actually getting into a car crash.

[ZACK. (Pulling back from her.) It's not going to happen again. You're over it.]

CAITLIN. *(Still chatty, still buoyantly happy.)* I'm not over it. You're going to have to take the wheel at some point. You know it's recently occurred to me, maybe it's not so strange, to have a panic attack in this situation. Maybe something in my brain knows something I don't know; maybe it's protecting me and being very sensible, very rational. I mean, up until this century human beings didn't go faster than, what, five miles an hour, unless they were flung up on an ox or a horse or something, pitched out a castle window. For centuries, for millennia, humans have traveled very, very slowly. When you think about it, going sixty miles an hour, going *forty* miles an hour is a profoundly *unnatural* thing to do. *Insanely* dangerous. Maybe some part of my brain realizes this and says what the fuck are you doing out in this little tinny shitty metal box that can crumple like gum foil in an instant, flying, hurtling through space alongside of hundreds of other people in little tinny metal boxes many of whom are complete idiots, people who willingly kept Reagan in office for eight years, *morons* entrusted with these death machines simply by virtue of having passed a multiple choice test they can take over and over and over until they pass? It's insane. Really, people have panic attacks in very logical places — elevators, airplanes, cars — dangerous places. Maybe it's not panic, maybe it's preservation of the species, common sense, it's "Get your body out of here. This is a very, very *stupid* place for you to be."

THE MEMORY OF WATER

BY SHELAGH STEPHENSON

CATHERINE — 30s.

SYNOPSIS: The death of their mother, Vi, leaves Mary, Teresa and Catherine quarreling over the funeral arrangements, the men in their lives and their conflicting memories of their childhood. The play begins in a comic vein, but gradually the bickering between the sisters grows sharper. Mary is having an affair with a married man and believes she is pregnant. Teresa is angry, feeling that she is the only responsible member of the family. Catherine, the youngest, has bounced from man to man, feeling as if she is never heard. Vi's spirit haunts Mary's thoughts, offering unwanted opinions and her memories of the past. Mike, Mary's boyfriend, and Frank, Teresa's husband, are unwilling participants in these fights. As tensions mounts, long-unspoken secrets of the family are revealed, and the fragile relationships between these people are pulled and stretched by the end of the play. Perhaps beyond the limit.

CATHERINE. Fuck it! *(Silence. She bursts into racking sobs.)* I went to this counselor — did I tell you this? — or a therapist or something and she said I had this problem and the problem was, I give too much, I just do too much for other people, I'm just a very giving person, and I never get any credit for any of it. I haven't even got any friends. I mean, I have but I don't like most of them, especially the women, and I try really hard, it's just I'm very sensitive and I get taken for a ride, nothing, ever goes right, every time, I mean, every time it's the same — like with men. What is it with men? I mean, I don't have a problem with men or anything. I love

69

men. I've been to bed with seventy-eight of them, I counted, so obviously there's not a problem or anything, it's just he didn't even apologize or anything and how can he say on the phone he doesn't want to see me anymore? I mean, why now? Why couldn't he have waited? I don't know what to do, why does it always go wrong? I don't want to be on my own, I'm sick of people saying I'll be better off on my own, I'm not that sort of person, I can't do it. I did everything for him, I was patient and all the things you're supposed to be and people kept saying don't accept this from him, don't accept that, like, you know, when he stayed out all night, not very often, I mean once or twice, and everyone said tell him to fuck off, but how could I because what if he did? Because they all do, everyone I've ever met does, they all disappear and I don't know if it's me or what. I don't want to be on my own, I can't stand it, I know it's supposed to be great but I don't think it is. I can't help it, it's no good pretending, it's fucking lonely and I can't bear it.

MERCY

BY LAURA CAHILL

ISOBEL — 20s.

SYNOPSIS: On Manhattan's Upper West Side, Sarah decides to brighten her spirits, and those of her friend Isobel, by throwing an impromptu dinner party. Sarah invites Bo, a wanna-be singer who, to the the dismay of Isobel, invites Stu, Isobel's ex-boyfriend. Isobel is deeply depressed over the break-up. She can barely look at Stu when he arrives, but, fighting through tears, she seeks only understanding and compassion from him. Feeling betrayed, Isobel has no other option but to wrestle her demons while feigning cordiality and contentment in the face of Sarah and Bo. Soon, the dinner party develops into an awkward facade of lost souls whose failure to communicate and find happiness has left them pitiful, hopelessly lonely and at the mercy of others.

ISOBEL. I'm so, so, so much better off with out him I mean god, could you imagine? He's such an asshole. He doesn't really believe in anything which is why I guess he could never believe me. He never seemed to believe anything I said. Especially when I was trying to tell him how I felt. He would just look down and say, "You cannot feel that way," or he would laugh. He really would, he would laugh and I'd say, "Why are you laughing at my feelings? I mean everybody knows you're not supposed to do that and that someone's feelings are their feelings and they can't be right or wrong." There's no right or wrong feelings everyone knows that. And he'd say, "I have to laugh because you can't possibly really feel that way," or "I don't understand." He'd say, "I don't understand," to like everything I would say. He wouldn't respond. There would never be any back and forth. And then last time I talked to hi started to cross the street! We were on 8th Avenue and h

71

started to cross the street while I was between two sentences. So I go with him across the street and he said, "I'm gonna go in there and get a bagel for the morning." So he got a couple of plain bagels in a little white bag and he was just holding it. All prepared. While I was feeling like ... so I finished my sentence and then he got in a cab. He's awful. He's so awful. I'm so happy I'm not with him. He's ... I don't know if there are words. I don't know if I could put it in a sentence, you know? How he is.

THE MINEOLA TWINS

BY PAULA VOGEL

MYRNA — 30s, the "good" twin.

SYNOPSIS: Myrna and Myra are identical twins but complete opposites. Myrna is the good twin, and she's stacked. Myra, on the other hand, is the bad twin, and she doesn't have as much in the chestal area. The sisters battle each other first over Myrna's boyfriend, Jim, and later over Myrna's son, Kenny, from the virginal Eisenhower era to Nixon's war in Vietnam and on through to George Bush's family values.

MYRNA. You know the story of the Prodigal Son? This man had two sons, right, and one worked hard in the fields from dawn to dusk. He never gave his parents cause to worry. The other son was a real *fuck-up*. I'm sorry, no other word will do. He never saved one thin dime, and he drank whatever money he filched from the family business. The Prodigal Son got into trouble with the law. He had to hide in this foreign land far across the borders, and a price was on his head. And he thought — wait a minute, I'll bet I can get Mom sorry for me, and she'll dip into the old man's pockets when he's asleep. And so he came dragging home in clothes that hadn't been washed in weeks. And his aged parents bailed him out. They drew his bath water. They washed his clothes. And they barbecued up filet mignon. And do you know what the Good Son felt, when he came home from the fields and saw his evil brother getting the ticker-tape parade? *What am I, ground chuck?*
[...]
MYRNA. The Good Brother bided his time, and then went to the cops in the other country and turned his sorry brother in. Took

the reward, and invested it. And then, he got control of his father's business. He sent his parents to a nice, clean nursing home where they had arts therapy. And when the Prodigal Son was finally released from the hoosegow, he had to beg in the marketplace, until the Prodigal Son finally *died*. And the Good Son danced and danced. Happy Ending!

THE MOST FABULOUS STORY EVER TOLD

BY PAUL RUDNICK

SHARON — a rabbi in a wheelchair, Sharon is an aggressively confident, gung-ho woman, a cable TV diva with a mission. She is stylishly dressed and coiffed.

SYNOPSIS: A stage manager, headset and prompt book at hand, brings the house lights out and cues the creation of the world. Act One recounts the major episodes of the Old Testament, with a twist: instead of Adam and Eve, our lead characters are Adam and Steve, and Jane and Mabel, a lesbian couple with whom they decide to start civiliza- tion. Along the way, Mabel and Adam invent God, but Jane and Steve are skeptical. This brings about the Flood, during which Steve has an affair with a rhinoceros and invents infidelity. No longer blissful, Adam and Steve break up only to be reunited as two of the wise men at the Nativity. Act Two jumps to modern-day Manhattan. Adam and Steve are together again, and Steve is HIV-positive. It's Christmas Eve, and Jane is nine months pregnant. The two women want to marry and want Adam and Steve to join them in the ceremony. Sharon, a wheelchair-bound, Jewish lesbian rabbi arrives to officiate. The cere- mony is interrupted as Jane gives birth, and Steve confides to Adam that his medication isn't working and he probably won't survive much longer. Bound by their long life together, and the miracle of birth they've witnessed, the men comfort each other, though they know their remaining time together will be short.

SHARON. [...] Siddown! [...] *(Gesturing to her wheelchair.)* I am. [...] Five years ago, it's Sunday morning, and I'm walking do~~ Christopher Street, on my legs. And I've just done a bat mitzv~

75

for my gorgeous niece, and I'm carrying my latte, my heavenly date-nut scone and the Sunday *Times*, and I'm headed back to see my naked young girlfriend. And then — a bicycle messenger. Outta nowhere, he swipes me, my legs go out, the *Times* goes flying, and I'm slammed smack — into the back of a FedEx truck. Which doesn't see me, so, as I'm lying in the street with a broken hip and five fractured ribs, it backs up onto my pelvis. FedEx truck tires! And then — it goes forward, right in my rib cage — crack! And by this point, people are screaming and pointing and then, and I swear, I am not making this up, I am a person of God — a rusty air conditioner falls off a twenty-story building, onto my face! And, as I finally lose consciousness, thank you, I see that bicycle messenger *eating my scone!*

And I come to, three weeks later, paralyzed, half-blind, and I think, what the fuck is going on? Not just why me, but why the fucking air conditioner? And some nurse gives me this book, called *Why Do Bad Things Happen to Good People*. And all I'm thinking is, I don't care! What I want to know is, why do *good* things happen to *bad* people! I'm in a wheelchair, and Saddam Hussein's in a Mercedes. I can't walk, and O.J.'s on the ninth hole. I'm paralyzed, and Brooke Shields has a series!

And then — it hits me. What doesn't? Why it happened. And what I'm supposed to do, with my useless legs and my messed-up life and my deluxe new nose — do you like it? *(She gestures to her nose.)* "The Mindy." So I buy me some airtime and I say, listen up, New York! Take a look! *(She gestures to herself and her wheelchair.)* This is your nightmare! This is the ice on the sidewalk, the maniac in the hallway, this is God when she's drunk! So if I can still believe, if I can still thank someone or something for each new day, if I can pee into a bag and still praise heaven for the pleasure, then so the fuck can all of you, mazel tov, praise Allah and amen!

NEW YORK ACTOR

BY JOHN GUARE

THE CRITIC'S WIFE.

SYNOPSIS: Several actors are sitting in a theater bar, reveling in success and failure — their own and that of their friends around them. Craig is back in New York after several seasons in Hollywood in a sitcom. So happy to be cast in an upcoming Broadway production, he doesn't mind revealing that Hollywood was not what he liked. The other stage actors agree but would have loved the chance to do TV. The uncertainty of their profession is personified by the theater critic and his wife seated at a nearby table, and the reality of it is driven home when another actor stops by and tells them of a Broadway part he just got, and they all realize Craig's been fired, and this guy is taking the role. Instead of rallying around, everyone goes their own way, leaving Craig with his greatest fear of being a has-been.

THE CRITIC'S WIFE. I hung my purse over the chair. *(Down on all fours looking under the table.)* It had everything in it. Keys. Money. *(Suddenly stops and looks out at us.)* I hate the theater. I hate the theater more than anything. I hate the contempt with which the little man at the door rips your ticket. I hate the little glossy program the usher hands you filled with pieces raving how wonderful the theater is. I hate it when I sit and look at the curtain on the stage. The dread of what lifting it is going to reveal. I hate it when there isn't a curtain. That? That's what I'm going to have to look at all night? I hate the people around me. I hate it when the audience applauds actors the moment they come out on stage. I hate seeing the makeup line at the actor's neck. I hate the artificial way actors talk. I hate the way they signal with their hands and mouths and bodies that a laugh line is coming up. I hate the way they freeze to hold for a laugh that never comes from me. I hate it when they burst into song. Most of all I hate it when actors look into the audience and talk to me as if I was their friend. I don't want actors revealing their innermost secrets, their so-called motives, their ludicrous hopes, laying out their noble dreams whose only purpose is to be crushed. Somebody else wrote their shoddy little secrets anyway. I hate playwrights. I hate directors. I hate the lighting. I hate the scenery. I wanted to marry a war correspondent. I thought I did. We met in Beirut during the war. In those days, he was a stringer for a weekly news magazine. I was on a TV crew. The two of us dreamed of a future of war zones, battlefields, civil insurrection. Fixing meals on hot plates in Mideast hotel rooms, making love in Israel as bombs go off over our heads, plaster falling down on us in joyous affirmation of our life. A tent in Bosnia. Watching him type his cogent reports on a beat-up portable Olivetti while I stayed back in the narrow cot, looking at him with pride. Smoking non-filters. Dreaming of the Spanish Civil War. Instead we came back to New York. Some chance of a lifetime. I'm held prisoner by a deranged kleptomaniac actor under a table looking for my keys in a show biz bar, lined with posters of flops. Everything's a flop. *Hamlet*'s a flop. *The Oresteia*'s a flop. *Hedda Gabler*'s a flop. *The Cherry Orchard*'s a flop. *Death of a Salesman*'s a flop. Me? Me? What am I?

OFF THE MAP

BY JOAN ACKERMANN

ARLENE — early 40s.

SYNOPSIS: Bo Groden looks back on the summer when she was eleven and everything changed. She sifts through the memories of an unusual childhood spent in the wilds of northern New Mexico where her enterprising parents forged a rich life off the land and the local dump. Desperate to escape as a child, longing for modern amenities and normalcy, now she yearns to go back. This is the summer when Charley, her father, spiraled into depression. Usually able to build and fix anything, he is unable to fix himself, but the family carries on, thanks to the earthy strength of Arlene, Bo's resourceful mother. Lonely for her father's companionship, Bo amuses herself by writing letters for free samples and praying for a miracle to deliver her from a mother who gardens in the nude and a father who cannot stop weeping. The miracle arrives in the form of William Gibbs, a displaced IRS agent who arrives in a fever and never leaves. As the artist within William emerges, each member of the family is touched and affected. By the time a boat arrives at the end of the play, the family's sails have been filled.

ARLENE. Oh God no. Charley! Not again, for Christ's sake. Charley! Come out of there! Come out! Now!! Enough! You can't spend another night in there! Charley! Look, you can lock yourself in the bedroom, you can lock yourself in the chicken house, the pig house, the barn, the car, no not the car and not the outhouse, come out of the outhouse now!! Where do you expect Bo and me to pee! Where do you expect your daughter to pee! We've got a sick boy in the house burning up with fever, a visitor, the least we should be able to offer him is a decent place to shit!! Now come out! You're being selfish, Charley, selfish, you're just sitting there, listening to me, just sitting there, being selfish and self-indulgent and self-pitying!! I God. *(She lies down, flat on her back, crosses her arms over her face. ... Softer.)* Charley. I can't take this much more. Sweetheart. Humility, Charley; it keeps you from being humiliated. That's where the word humiliation comes from. Everybody gets depressed some time, why should you be above it. *(She sits up; sighs.)* I'll say this for you, when you take on a project, you give it your all. You've never done anything half-assed, and you're not doing it now. *(Pause.)* I've been thinking, maybe we should try to have another kid. We're getting kind of old for it, but ... She can't stay a little girl forever, Charley. Just cause she's growing up doesn't mean we're losing her. [...] There's some food out here. *(Pause.)* I'm sorry I yelled at you. Sweetheart. *(Pause.)* Charley? *(Fearing the worst.)* Charley, say something!

THE OLD SETTLER

BY JOHN HENRY REDWOOD

QUILLY — a black woman, 53 years old.

SYNOPSIS: In World War II Harlem, New York, a fifty-five-year-old spinster (or as they were called in those days — an "Old Settler.") Elizabeth Borny, takes in a young male roomer, Husband Witherspoon, to help her with the rent. Husband has come to Harlem from South Carolina to search for his girlfriend, Lou Bessie Preston. Also living with Elizabeth is her sister, Quilly McGrath, fifty-three. There is an ominous cloud of tension that hangs over Elizabeth and Quilly's relationship. This tension is further exacerbated when Elizabeth and Husband take to liking each other. Quilly, who doesn't like Husband living with them in the first place, surely doesn't approve of their "carrying on," especially since Elizabeth is old enough to be Husband's mother. It is this "carrying on" that exposes a thirty-year-old wound which, until now, only had a bandage — now the wound can heal for the sisters.

QUILLY. You remember how Sister Wallace at the church was so happy because she and her four children was going down to Georgia to spend Mother's Day with her mama?
[ELIZABETH. Yeah.]
QUILLY. She hadn't seen her mama in six years. The poor woman had been saving all year to get the train fare. Me and some of the other people at the church even fried chicken and baked biscuits and cornbread and cake and put it in shoe boxes so they could have something to eat on the train. Well, they left last night. But when we got to church this morning, Reverend Osborne told us that Sister Wallace had called his house crying. Seems when they got to Washington, D.C., her and those children had to get out of

the car they was sitting in and move back to the colored cars at the end of the train. But there was only two colored cars and all those colored folks couldn't fit in just those two cars. Now, those greedy crackers had done overbooked the whole train. So when white folks didn't have seats in the all-white cars, the railroad would charge them half price if they would be willing to ride the colored car. And if they were, a colored person had to get up and let the cracker have their seat. If there were too many colored people standing in the aisle, they'd make some of them get off the train. They kept letting white folks on and kept kicking Negroes off until there was no room for Sister Wallace and those four children. So now she's stuck in Washington, D.C., with a little bit of money and a couple of shoe boxes of fried chicken and cornbread.

[ELIZABETH. *Lord have mercy. What's she going to do?*]

QUILLY. [*How am I supposed to know?*] As of an hour ago, she and them children were still sitting in the colored waiting room. She's not going to make it to Georgia for Mother's Day, I know that. I don't know what make white folks so mean.

OUR LADY OF SLIGO

BY SEBASTIAN BARRY

MARIA — 60, square-bodied, bright open face.

SYNOPSIS: From her hospital bed in 1950s Dublin, Mai O'Hara recalls her life through morphine-induced memories and hallucinations. Dying of liver cancer caused by alcoholism, Mai reminisces on her youthful promise as a member of the Galway bourgeoisie; the death of one of her children; of the marriage fueled by liquor, bickering, and remorse, to her husband, Jack; and of fleeing to the home of her cousin Maria when Jack's drinking was at its worst. Jack's visits to her bedside are a testament to the mutual hatred they share and the mutual dependence they have on each other. Through it all, Mai uses her mordant wit and vanity to pull her out of painful realizations. Once the first woman in Sligo to wear trousers, it emerges that Mai is not only the victim of a broken marriage, but a victim of an Ireland in which the Catholic middle-class has been nullified by spiritual and political isolation after the Civil War.

MARIA.   Look, Mai, you're a young woman still and all your life ahead of you. To speak plainly, I've seen old bachelor farmers about here start to drink and it never suits them. You'll find one or other of such men any Sunday morning strewn about at the crossroads, or heaped into a ditch, their bicycle near them like a faithful dog. And they've been driving down the drink in Kilnaleck all night and that's their life, and rarely do they take out a scythe to keep the grass down in the haggard, and I don't know how they live, except Nicholas gives them a job now and then, in the season. But whether they start as a man of a hundred acres or a man with none, it all comes to the same thing in the end, a broken-bodied and brokenhearted man like a handful of embers in the county home, and when they die they pass away like the mark of rain on the earth when the sun returns. Child of grace, take heed of my words, and bestir yourself, and love your child. You were born to the best of everything and it seems to me the world of drinking is too dark and strange for little ones.

[MAI. It is, doubtless.]

MARIA.   So fix your boat, Mai, and think of your father that you loved so well.

[MAI. I do think of him, often, believe me.]

MARIA.   That's all I can think to say to you. I have five decent-minded cows to relieve of their milk. You'll forgive me.

OURSELVES ALONE

BY ANNE DEVLIN

DONNA — friend to both sisters, Liam's common-law wife, under 30.

SYNOPSIS: Three women in Belfast dream of escaping the political peril that marks their lives, but cannot because of the family loyalties instilled in them and their complicated relationships with men. Frieda is a would-be singer whose pro-IRA father disowns her, sending her into the arms of a Workers' Party organizer and anti-IRA zealot. Her sister Josie is in love with an IRA leader, but ends up carrying the child of another man. And Donna, who waits five years for her lover to emerge from prison and finds that the overbearing and unfaithful man wasn't worth the wait.

DONNA. The devil's back. He was lying with his head on my pillow this morning. When I woke up I recognized him immediately. Even though it's been years. *(Pause.)* The first time I ever saw him, he was standing in the corner of the room. I could feel something watching me. I had the bedclothes tucked up almost to my nose, so that I had to peer carefully round the room — and there he was. He seemed to grow out of the corner until he was towering over me. I panicked because I felt I was suffocating. My first husband was with me at the time. He called a doctor. He said I had asthma. The funny thing was, I really didn't get over my asthma attacks until my husband was interned. And I haven't seen the devil since. *(Pause.)* Until this morning. Liam bent over and kissed me goodbye as he was leaving. The trouble was he blocked my mouth and I couldn't breathe through my nose so I kept having to break away from him. When he'd gone, I closed my eyes and tried to get some sleep before the child woke. That was when I heard the door open.

85

I thought Liam had come back so I opened my eyes, and there he was, the devil. If he had any hair at all it was red. He climbed on top of the bed and put his head on the pillow next to me. I felt so sick at the sight of him because I knew I didn't have the strength to struggle anymore. I said: "Please leave me alone." I was very surprised when he replied. He's never spoken to me before. He said very quietly, "All right, Donna." And do you know — he vanished. But I don't believe he's really gone. He never really goes away.

PLAN DAY

BY LESLIE AYVAZIAN

WOMAN — 40s.

SYNOPSIS: One woman plays a mother to her only child, a son, in four stages of her life: her 30s, 40s, 50s and 70s. Each monologue begins with "lights up" and ends with "blackout." This connotes the beginning and end of a day, as each decade passes and her love for her son ages and ripens.

WOMAN.
Okay.
Day's here. Get up!
Get a job. Answer ads. Polish shoes. Practice interview.
Plan day.
Don't sit for too long.
Don't sit in this chair with your back to the window.
Don't stare. Don't let go of this coffee cup. Don't put your feet
    up. Don't settle in. Get the paper off the lawn. Wash your
    socks. Wash this robe. Wash your hair.
Learn something new.
Volunteer ... nah.
Meet new people. Join a group. Join a support group! Join a sup-
    port group for divorced-mothers-whose-son-is-a-teenager.
Yes!

No. Join a support group for women who spend the day in blue
bathrobes and gray socks, drinking one cup of coffee that goes
from warm to cold. For women whose hands go from warm to
cold as the hands hold the cup that holds the coffee that loses its
heat. And the hands stay on the cup and the feet stay on the

ottoman and the shadows grow long across the room and the papers stay on the lawn. That's the group for me.

Or. I'll find a group for divorced women with one son who can't cook! Every day, cruising the Supermarket, watching other women's carts. Even asking: "Excuse me — hi! — You mind my asking ... What are you making for dinner? ... Sausage and green peppers? ... What's in that?" There's the support group I need!

And my son can join a group for Children of Noodles!
Children of Just Noodles.
Or Children of Noodles, and a side of sausage and peppers that's thrown away. A support group for children who had to throw away half of what was on their plate every night, because it was not edible!

So, that's the group for me and for my son. Lousy food, poor nutrition. No visible effect on health, though. There's the upside. After the first five years of turned-in feet and soft teeth and reactive airways, not much to contend with. Only eighty-seven pox with the chicken pox! Lorraine Bonavitch had several hundred; eyes, vagina, awful. There should be a group for mothers with children who have over one hundred pox.

And a group for mothers to attend when their children are out at night. A group for mothers who hold vigil through all the teenage years. There's the perfect group! Women waiting together. Waiting for him to walk back in the door — clear-eyed. Happy.

THE RIDE DOWN MOUNT MORGAN

BY ARTHUR MILLER

THEO — 50s, married to Lyman.

SYNOPSIS: Lyman's desires have allowed him to believe that loving — and marrying — two women at the same time is the kind of love that is totally truthful and that he is being true to himself. When found out, his wives, Theo and the younger Leah, clarify the position: Only by deceiving everyone has he found a way to his own false sense of truth. While lying in the hospital, recovering from bad injuries after a car crash, Lyman's wives meet. They are shocked and devastated, as are the children who once adored Lyman, and now verge on despising him. As we follow the chain of events that lead up to this day, what is revealed is a selfish man, willing to take, while others around him are willing to give and to turn a blind's eye to suspicions. We also feel the indictment of a society that urges us to give meaning to our life by individually defining it only for ourselves. In the end, Lyman is left by those who once loved him, and he must face the loneliness he now knows is his real, true self.

THEO. *(To Leah.)* I wish I hadn't carried on that way … I'm sorry. I've really nothing against you personally, I just never cared for your type. The surprise is what threw me, I mean that you were actually married. But I think you are rather an interesting person. … I was just unprepared, but I'm seeing things much clearer now. Yes. *(Breaks off.)* Do you see the *Village Voice* up here?
[…]
THEO. There was a strange interview some years back with Isaac Bashevis Singer, the novelist? The interviewer was a woman whose

89

husband had left her for another woman, and she couldn't understand why. And Singer said, "Maybe he liked her hole better." I
was shocked at the time, really outraged — you know, that he'd
gotten a Nobel; but now I think it was courageous to have said
that, because it's probably true. Courage ... courage and directness
are always the main thing!

[...]

THEO. I can't remember if I called you Leah or Mrs. Felt.

[...]

THEO. *(With a pleasant social smile.)* Well, you are a Mrs. Felt;
perhaps that's all one can hope for when we are so interchangeable
— who knows anymore which Mrs. Felt will be coming down for
breakfast! *(Short pause.)* Your boy needs his father, I imagine.

[...]

THEO. Then he should be here with you, shouldn't he. We must
all be realistic now. *(To Lyman.)* You can come up here whenever
you want to ... if that's what you'd really like.

[...]

THEO. I'm not at all ill; *(To Lyman.)* I can say "fuck" you know.
I never cared for the word but I'm sure she has her limitations too.
I can say "fuck me, Lyman," "fuck you, Lyman"; whatever.

SCENT OF THE ROSES

BY LISETTE LECAT ROSS

ANNALISE MORANT — a white woman in her late 60s.

SYNOPSIS: An international art dealer arrives in South Africa in search of early works by an exiled painter. Annalise Morant, a South African woman, owns just such a work — a landscape, her most cherished possession. For reasons of their own, her children are eager for her to meet with the dealer; but when she does, it sets in motion a swift series of events sending her on an emotional and physical journey — forcing her to come to terms with a past that has haunted her, to redress a wrong before it's too late. A story of the resilience of memory, the choices framed by circumstance, about love and loss, SCENT OF THE ROSES captures the essence of the new and the old South Africa in all its heartbreaking complexity.

ANNALISE. I want to tell you our story. In the beginning. When we shared a story … *(Beat.)* When I knew that you were there, I was deathly afraid. What I had done, what had happened, was a crime. An immoral act. It said so in the statute books. And we would go to jail. That was the law, back in the fifties. *(Beat.)* So scared … For you would be the living proof that I had done this deed. And was a criminal. White woman who'd loved a man who wasn't. Who never knew he'd fathered you. Your warm and cinnamon-colored skin, soft and smooth as rose petals. As you lay asleep in my arms. So beautiful. Perdita. My lost one. First child. The one I gave away. He had gone. Your father. I was alone with this big, big secret. And what to do? If they knew, it would ruin my parents. My mother would die for the shame of it. I had to get rid of these cells inside me. That, too, was against the law. Officially the lesser crime. They couldn't judge a thimbleful of cells. But where

91

to go? A squalid back street? I didn't know another way. Some horrid stranger. ... Destroying you? I couldn't. Couldn't do that. And all this while you were there inside me: changing, unfolding, becoming you. Bound and determined. You and my body in special partnership. According to some infinitely greater laws. So I did the only thing I could. I left my world and entered the one that would one day be yours. Astonishing how easily I could navigate, how quickly the connections formed. In that world. Where this was just an everyday catastrophe. Where details and documents were a haphazard affair. Back there, three women only shared my secret. *(Wonders at it.)* And kept it ... And so I left Slade River. I went back to the College. Found a room in a boardinghouse, went to lectures, to the library, went shopping, did my laundry, tried to concentrate. Hid your growing presence under shapeless clothes ... The days had no validity...! And in the dark and sleepless nights I tried to tell you everything. Enough to last a lifetime. And made my hopeless plans to keep you. The more impossible they were, the more obsessive they became. And how I hated the men who'd made those laws. Made our act of love a crime so reprehensible. With all my heart I hated them. And how I loved you. My overwhelming secret. Lying, curled inside me, listening. My only friend. My child I would betray. And remember till I draw my last breath.

SNAKEBIT

BY DAVID MARSHALL GRANT

JENIFER — 30s.

SYNOPSIS: A study of modern friendship when put to the test, the play centers on Jonathan and his wife Jenifer while they visit their oldest friend, Michael, at his home in Los Angeles. Jonathan, an actor, is in L.A. auditioning for a film — his first big break at stardom — and he's dragged Jenifer with him for support. Jenifer is distant because their daughter was left at home with a relative and she's become ill. Michael is distracted since his boyfriend has left him and one of the children he counsels was beaten and put in a hospital where he cannot see her. At first the focus is on the universal questions we all face at one point or another, specifically self-doubt, and our selfish need for support. With the arrival of a guest, the play becomes deeper and forces us to see how ugly we can be when we look only at ourselves when we really should remember to look at others — especially those we love.

JENIFER.   I don't want to be an actress. I hate acting. I've always hated acting. It fills me with nothing but self-loathing. There, I said it. And you know, you do your affirmations, you know, your prayers that you'll be like, you know, so filled with self-love, that all that won't matter. What am I saying? The whole thing's a joke. You know why I don't want to act? And don't tell Jonathan this. I've never told anybody this. I started to stutter. On stage. Can you believe that? Honestly. I would get to a word in the script, and when I came to it, I wouldn't be able to say it. I would freeze. Every time I would get to it. I couldn't get it out.
[MICHAEL.   You started to stutter?]
JENIFER.   I get fixated on a word. Last time, I was playing the blind Mexican flower vendor in *Streetcar Named Desire.* Don't ask

me why. And all I had to do was say, *"Flores para los muertos."* There, I said it now. *"Flores para los muertos."* I had nothing else to say, just that. I sat around waiting all night. *"Flores para los muertos." "Flores para los muertos."* I couldn't say it. Now I can say it. It's pathetic.

[MICHAEL. What couldn't you say?]

JENIFER. *Muertos.* I couldn't say, *Muertos.* It wouldn't come out. I ended up saying, *"Flores para los* dead people." Blanche DuBois accused me of sabotaging her performance.

[MICHAEL. Well, fuck her. You adapted under difficult circumstances. What did she want you to do? Not say anything?]

JENIFER. She wanted me to say the line right. That's what I was not getting paid to do. And Jonathan made me feel so … You know, why don't I just leave him? I really should just leave him.

STOP KISS

BY DIANA SON

CALLIE — late 20s to early 30s.

SYNOPSIS: A poignant and funny play about the ways, both sudden and slow, that lives can change irrevocably. After Callie meets Sara, the two unexpectedly fall in love. But their first kiss provokes a violent attack from a man on the street that leaves Sara in a coma. Callie struggles to make sense of it all as she deals with her friends, Sara's medical condition, a police detective investigating the assault, and her own conflicted emotions.

CALLIE. Because we were kissing. *(Det. Cole gestures — there it is.)* It was the first — We didn't know he was there. Until he said something. "Hey, save some of that for me." Sara told him to leave us alone. I couldn't believe she — then he offered to pay us. He said he'd give us fifty bucks if we went to a motel with him and let him watch. He said we could dry hump or whatever we like to do — turns him on just to see it. I grabbed her arm and started walking away. He came after us, called us fucking dykes — pussy-eating dykes. Sara told him to fuck off. I couldn't believe — he came up and punched her in the back, then he grabbed her and pulled her away. I yelled for someone to call the police. He pushed her against the building and started banging her head against the building. He told her to watch her cunt-licking mouth. But he had his hand over her jaw, she couldn't — she just made these mangled — she was trying to breathe. I came up behind him and grabbed his hair — he turned around and punched me in the stomach. I threw up, it got on him. Sara tried to get away but he grabbed her and started banging her head against his knee. I tried to hold his arms back but he was stronger — he knocked her out. He pushed me to the

95

ground and started kicking me. Someone yelled something — "cops are coming" — and he took off in the opposite direction. West. He was limping. He hurt his knee. *(She looks at Det. Cole.)* That's what happened.

STUPID KIDS

BY JOHN C. RUSSELL

JANE "KIMBERLY" WILLIS — 17, lonely, angry, queer.

SYNOPSIS: In rapid, highly stylized, music video–like scenes, STUPID KIDS follows four students at Joe McCarthy High School as they make their way from first through eighth period and beyond, struggling with the fears, frustrations and longings peculiar to youth. Jim is the new guy in town, sexy, a rebel. Judy is the popular blonde cheerleader. Neechee and Kimberly are the resident outcasts, both of whom are secretly gay. Will Jim become popular? Will Judy give her virginity to Jim? Will Neechee and Kimberly confess they're gay? With his magical touch, John C. Russell turns these familiar stereotypes into deeply moving and provocative archetypes of adolescence whose jocular lingo takes on a lyricism that is both true to its source and astonishingly revelatory of the hearts and minds of contemporary youth.

KIMBERLY.   "A Letter to Judy."
This letter is a poem because
I cannot make my feelings into grammar
I want the back-front-up-down-in-out-North-South-through-the-
      chimney-
down-the-drainpipe-any-damn-way-you-please journey of poetry
to take me through my longing for you
We share secrets and cigarettes
laughter and lingerie
tears hopes dreams desires
But I fear my desire for you far exceeds your expectations
We move in different orbits
A true collision could destroy the universe
But still I think maybe it could be beautiful

Explosions of the fireworks kind
Red boom blue boom white boom green boom purple boom
boom boom boom boom boom
And there'd be a new beginning
A new world
A new us

Yours most deeply.

UNCLE VANYA

BY BRIAN FRIEL
FROM THE PLAY BY ANTON CHEKHOV

ELANA — aged 27. The wife of Alexander Serebryakov, a retired professor.

SYNOPSIS: Two lives, those of Uncle Vanya and his niece Sonya, are at the core of this play. They work their small estate, live frugally and keep their emotions tightly reined in. Then they are visited by a relative, Professor Serebryakov, and his beautiful young wife, Elena. Vanya falls helplessly in love with Elena, Sonya with a local doctor — and their lives implode.

ELENA.   People shouldn't burden you with their secrets when there's nothing you can do about them. Because he's not in love with her — that's obvious to everybody but her. Of course that doesn't mean that he couldn't marry her. She has a sweet nature and she'd be an excellent wife for a country doctor who's not exactly a boy anymore. Because she's bright and she's considerate and she's — diligent, that's the word — as if any of that matters in the slightest. And why wouldn't she be restless in this damned — quagmire? You know exactly how she feels, don't you? Oh, indeed you do: rising, talking, eating, sleeping; the thrilling pattern of our lives day in, day out, seven days a week. So that picking gooseberries is an occasion. A new roof on the granary is an event. The arrival of the thresher — good God, that is a Greek drama! And then he appears — aloof— engaged — diffident — arrogant. And of course she's spellbound. In this setting he's almost exotic, isn't he? So that when he appears, the day suddenly has that little frisson, that whiff of unease, that scent of danger, doesn't it? And listening to you, Elena, I suspect you're not altogether immune yourself. Why are you smiling? Vanya says you have mermaid blood in your veins, doesn't he? So why not take that plunge into the wine-dark sea? Why not? And in that defiant plunge escape forever from this damned prison and all the prisoners in it? Why not indeed? Because you're too cowardly and too timid. Even though you know in your heart why he comes here every day now, don't you? Oh, yes, you know very well. So really you should be asking Sonya to forgive you, shouldn't you?

THE UNEASY CHAIR

BY EVAN SMITH

ALEXANDRINA CROSIBE DARLINGTON — 20s/30s, extraordinarily fashionable.

SYNOPSIS: Somewhere in the nineteenth century, Amelia Pickles, a prim and proper spinster of modest means, agrees to let out a room in her Victorian London establishment to a retired military man, Josiah Wickett. The arrangement seems to be working out until Mr. Wickett decides to play matchmaker with Miss Pickles' prissy niece Alexandrina, and his nephew, Darlington, an officer in the cavalry. Through a gross misinterpretation, Miss Pickles believes she, not Alexandrina, is the object of Mr. Wickett's, not Darlington's, affection. Miss Pickles is convinced Mr. Wickett will soon ask for her hand in marriage. When he denies, she decides to take her boarder to a court of law for breach of promise. Mr. Wickett loses the trial. Or does he win? He doesn't wish to pay Miss Pickles her settlement and instead he opts to marry the lonely woman. Through the musings, regrets, anecdotes and comedic bickerings between their forced duet it seems as though just maybe they were meant to be together after all.

ALEXANDRINA. Afterwards, I found it extremely difficult to explain how I stumbled into my disastrous marriage. [...] Of course, all of my friends and relations tried to convince me to retreat from my engagement, and I admit the urgency of this consensus made me somewhat rebellious. It is my nature that when all the world tells me to do A, I perversely yearn to do B, the perverse option B in this case being — but that is not a complete explanation of why I married Mr. Darlington. I do not believe I am more than moderately motivated by feelings of spite, and I openly confess I was sensible of those masculine charms he possessed independently of my desire to be contrary. [...] But more than these reasons was another. I had for some time previous felt myself in danger of becoming what people call shallow. What better way to prove the existence of unsuspected profundity than by marrying a man with no possible attraction than his own person? And even though I knew the feeling in my heart was most likely not that felt by passionate, profound women, I hoped the deed would evoke in me the emotion. And so I married.

THE VAGINA MONOLOGUES

BY EVE ENSLER

SYNOPSIS: THE VAGINA MONOLOGUES introduces a wildly divergent gathering of female voices, including a six-year-old girl, a septuagenarian New Yorker, a vagina workshop participant, a woman who witnesses the birth of her granddaughter, a Bosnian survivor of rape, and a feminist happy to have found a man who "liked to look at it."

MY ANGRY VAGINA

My vagina's angry. It is. It's pissed off. My vagina's furious and it needs to talk. It needs to talk about all this shit. It needs to talk to you. I mean what's the deal — an army of people out there thinking up ways to torture my poor-ass, gentle, loving vagina ... Spending their days constructing psycho products, and nasty ideas to undermine my pussy. Vagina Motherfuckers.

All this shit they're constantly trying to shove up us, clean us up — stuff us up, make it go away. Well, my vagina's not going away. It's pissed off and it's staying right here. Like tampons — what the hell is that? A wad of dry fucking cotton stuffed up there. Why can't they find a way to subtly lubricate the tampon? As soon as my vagina sees it, it goes into shock. It says forget it. It closes up. You need to work with the vagina, introduce it to things, prepare the way. That's what foreplay's all about. You got to convince my vagina, seduce my vagina, engage my vagina's trust. You can't do that with a dry wad of fucking cotton.

Stop shoving things up me. Stop shoving and stop cleaning it up.

My vagina doesn't need to be cleaned up. It smells good already. Don't try to decorate. Don't believe them when he tells you it smells like rose petals when it's supposed to smell like pussy. That's what they're doing, trying to clean it up, make it smell like bathroom spray or a garden. All those douche sprays, floral, berry, rain. I don't want my pussy to smell like rain. All cleaned up like washing a fish after you cook it. I want to taste the fish. That's why I ordered it.

VERNON EARLY

BY HORTON FOOTE

MILDRED EARLY — 50.

SYNOPSIS: VERNON EARLY revisits American life in Horton Foote's fictional town of Harrison, Texas, during the 1950s. The title character, Vernon, is a doctor, in the days when the house call was commonplace. Consumed by his work, his spirit has been eroded by the pressures of his job and the lingering depression he shares with his wife, Mildred, over the loss of their adopted child to his birth mother. Mirroring the tragic existence of the Earlys, many of Harrison's other residents are also consumed with the self-inflicted wounds of life: aging, individual isolation, love, and racial inequality. Through all of the bleakness of life there still shines a glimmer of hope reflected in the spirit of the town's sad doctor: Vernon Early.

MILDRED.   God knows. I pretend I don't care about that either. I hope we go to Bermuda, but he keeps eyeing some places in Mexico. *(She laughs.)* Not that it makes any difference where we go. He never leaves the ship. The last one we took together was to Bermuda, and when we docked I said I was going ashore to shop and he said he'd prefer waiting as usual on the ship. So off I go and wandered farther than I should and I decided I'd get a taxi, back to the ship, and I hailed one and got in and we rode a few blocks and it stopped and picked up another passenger, and we rode a few more blocks and we stopped and picked up another passenger and then another and by this time I was getting very nervous and anxious and I told the driver I had little time and he told me to relax and not worry, and he began driving to what seemed like a very strange section of the city and the driver stopped and let one passenger off and then another off and I looked at my watch and the time of departure for the boat was getting closer and closer and then he let another passenger off and then another and by this time I was in a panic, not only did I think I would miss the boat, but I was afraid he was taking me some place to rape me or rob me. And so I began to cry and pleaded with him to get me right to the boat and he turned the car around after giving me the most disgusted look and raced through the town and got me there just in time. My God I was very relieved. And Vernon was scared to death too, although he wouldn't admit it. He was standing on the deck looking at his watch.

THE WEIR

BY CONOR McPHERSON

VALERIE — 30s.

SYNOPSIS: In a bar in rural Ireland, the local men swap spooky stories in an attempt to impress Valerie, a young woman from Dublin who recently moved into a nearby "haunted" house. However, the tables are soon turned when she tells them a chilling story of her own.

VALERIE. And I gave her a little hug. She was freezing cold. And I told her Mammy loved her very much. She just looked asleep but her lips were gone blue and she was dead.

And it had happened so fast. Just a few minutes. And I don't think I have to tell you. How hard it was. Between me and Daniel, as well. It didn't seem real. At the funeral I just thought I could go and lift her out of the coffin and would be the end of all this.

I think Daniel was. I don't know if he actually, blamed me, there was nothing I could do. But he became very busy in his work. Just. Keeping himself ... em. But I was, you know, I was more, just I didn't really know what I was doing. Just walking around, wanting to ... Sitting in the house, with Daniel's mother, fussing around the place.

Just, months of this. Not really talking about it, like. *(Pause.)*

But, and then one morning. I was in bed, Daniel had gone to work. I usually lay there for a few hours, trying to stay asleep, really. I suppose. And the phone rang. And I just left it. I wasn't going to get it. And it rang for a long time. Em, eventually it stopped, and I was dropping off again. But then it started ringing again, for a long time. So I thought it must have been Daniel trying to get me. Someone who knew I was there.

So I went down and answered it. And. The line was very faint.

107

It was like a crossed line. There were voices, but I couldn't hear what they were saying. And then I heard Niamh. She said, "Mammy?" And I ... just said, you know, "Yes." *(Short pause.)*

And she said ... She wanted me to come and collect her. I mean, I wasn't sure whether this was a dream or her leaving us had been a dream. I just said, "Where are you?"

And she said she thought she was at Nana's. In the bedroom. But Nana wasn't there. And she was scared. There were children knocking in the walls and the man was standing across the road, and he was looking up and he was going to cross the road. And would I come and get her?

And I said I would, of course I would. And I dropped the phone and I ran out to the car in just a T-shirt I slept in. And I drove to Daniel's mother's house. And I could hardly see, I was crying so much. I mean, I knew she wasn't going to be there. I knew she was gone. But to think wherever she was ... that ... And there was nothing I could do about it.

Daniel's mother got a doctor and I ... slept for a day or two. But it was ... Daniel felt that I ... needed to face up to Niamh being gone. But I just thought that he should face up to what happened to me. He was insisting I get some treatment, and then ... everything would be okay. But you know, what can help that, if she's out there? She still ... she still needs me.

WIT

BY MARGARET EDSON

VIVIAN BEARING, PH.D. — 50; professor of seventeenth-century poetry at the university.

SYNOPSIS: Vivian Bearing, Ph.D., a renowned professor of English who has spent years studying and teaching the brilliant and difficult metaphysical sonnets of John Donne, has been diagnosed with terminal ovarian cancer. Her approach to the study of Donne: aggressively probing, intensely rational. But during the course of her illness — and her stint as a prize patient in an experimental chemotherapy program at a major teaching hospital — Vivian comes to reassess her life and her work with a profundity and humor that are transformative.

VIVIAN. That certainly was a *maudlin* display. Popsicles? "Sweetheart"? I can't believe my life has become so ... corny.

But it can't be helped. I don't see any other way. We are discussing life and death, and not in the abstract, either; we are discussing *my* life and *my* death, and my brain is dulling, and poor Susie's was never very sharp to begin with, and I can't conceive of any other ... *tone.*

(Quickly.) Now is not the time for verbal swordplay, for unlikely flights of imagination and wildly shifting perspectives, for metaphysical conceit, for wit.

And nothing would be worse than a detailed scholarly analysis. Erudition. Interpretation. Complication.

(Slowly.) Now is a time for simplicity. Now is a time for, dare I say it, kindness.

(Searchingly.) I thought being extremely smart would take care of it. But I see that I have been found out. Ooohhh.

I'm scared. Oh, God. I want ... I want ... No. I want to hide.

I just want to curl up in a little ball. (... *Vivian [is] in horrible pain. She is tense, agitated, fearful. Slowly she calms down and addresses the audience. Trying extremely hard.)*

I want to tell you how it feels. I want to explain it, to use *my* words. It's as if ... I can't ... There aren't ... I'm like a student and this is the final exam and I don't know what to put down because I don't understand the question and I'm *running out of time. (Pause.)*

The time for extreme measures has come. I am in terrible pain. Susie says that I need to begin aggressive pain management if I am going to stand it.

"It": such a little word. In this case, I think "it" signifies "being alive."

I apologize in advance for what this palliative treatment modality does to the dramatic coherence of my play's last scene. It can't be helped. They have to do something. I'm in terrible pain.

Say it, Vivian. *It hurts like hell. It really does.*

Oh, God. Oh, God.

WORKOUT

BY WENDY WASSERSTEIN

SYNOPSIS: In the course of a single WORKOUT, an exercise instructor writes on a novel, opens a chain of departments stores, learns to unravel the double helix and announces her husband's candidacy for governor.

WOMAN. Ready for your workout? We'll start with buttock tucks. These are my favorite. Now lie back, breathe deep. Big breath. Mmmmmm. Relax, feet forward. Remember, make the muscles burn. *(She begins to bounce her buttocks.)*

And lift and lower. And lift and lower. Squeeze it. Squeeze it. Push up, release. Push up and release. Really squeeze it, Denise. Lift up, lift up and bounce bounce bounce. *(She begins doing leg lifts.)*

This is what I like to think about when I'm doing my workout. I think about how I got up at four-thirty in the morning and ran for five miles. And how great that run felt. Keep bouncing, up down up down. I like to think about the brewer's yeast I gave my children for breakfast. Squeeze it! Squeeze it! And how proud I am that the words "French toast" are never used in our house. I think about my husband's stamina. It's better now than when we first got married because we're organized. Work deep. Work deep! *(She does lifts in fire hydrant position.)*

And I think about the novel I'm writing between nine and eleven this morning. And the chain of appliance stores I'm opening at twelve. I just think it's so important that we take charge of our own appliances. Last week I restored the electricity for the city of Fresno. And a year ago I couldn't use a can opener. Just keep bouncing, Denise. And one, and two. And this afternoon after my yogurt shake ... *(She goes into a split.)*

Ooooooooooooooh I felt the burn that time. I'm going to learn ancient Egyptian so I can star in the Nefertiti story, which I am also producing, directing, writing, editing and distributing. I'll need all my strength. Let's do twenty more. Denise, put the gun down. Your life isn't my fault! Be angry with your buttocks. Let them know your feelings. *(She squats, elbow to knee.)*

At five o'clock I'm going to my daughter's dance recital, where my husband will announce his candidacy for governor — I hope you all will vote for him — and I will announce the publication of my new workout book for children under six and their pets. On our way home, the entire family will stop at the home of a woman friend of mine for women's friendship and Tofutti ice cream. Release, release, we're almost there. Don't give in. Push it. Push it. *(She begins doing jumping jacks.)*

And then my very favorite part of the day. Tuck in. Feel it all over. The children are outside playing nonviolent baseball with radishes and zucchinis, my husband is preparing his part of the family meal and debating with Connie Chung and the six o'clock news team by satellite. Just two more. Get ready to release. And it is time for my moment. Just me. *(She stops exercising for the first time.)*

And I sit for the first time in the day. On my favorite chair, with my favorite quilt. And I take a deep breath, and I cry. *(She pauses.)* But just a little. *(She stands up.)*

And then I tuck in my stomach and pull up from the chair. Vertebra by vertebra. And I take a deep inhalation and exhale. And now we're ready for fifty more jumping jacks. And one, and two, and three, let's go, Denise. *(She continues jumping happily.)*

PERMISSIONS ACKNOWLEDGMENTS:

APARTMENT 3A by Jeff Daniels. Copyright © 2000, Jeff Daniels. Reprinted by permission of International Creative Management, 40 West 57th Street, New York, NY 10019 on the author's behalf.

THE BATTING CAGE by Joan Ackermann. Copyright © 1999, Joan Ackermann. Reprinted by permission of Harden-Curtis Associates, 850 Seventh Avenue, Suite 405, New York, NY 10019 on the author's behalf.

THE BEAUTY QUEEN OF LEENANE by Martin McDonagh. Copyright © 1996, 1999, Martin McDonagh. Reprinted by permission of The Rod Hall Agency Ltd., 3 Charlotte Mews, London W1T 4DZ, England on the author's behalf.

BETTY'S SUMMER VACATION by Christopher Durang. Copyright © 1999, 2000, Christopher Durang. Reprinted by permission of Helen Merrill Ltd., 295 Lafayette Street, Suite 915, New York, NY 10012 on the author's behalf.

BLUES FOR AN ALABAMA SKY by Pearl Cleage. Copyright © 1999, Pearl Cleage. Reprinted by permission of Rosenstone/Wender, 38 East 29th Street, New York, NY 10016 on the author's behalf.

BOOK OF DAYS by Lanford Wilson. Copyright © 2001, Lanford Wilson. Reprinted by permission of International Creative Management, 40 West 57th Street, New York, NY 10019 on the author's behalf.

COLLECTED STORIES by Donald Margulies. Copyright © 1998, Donald Margulies. Reprinted by permission of Rosenstone/Wender, 38 East 29th Street, New York, NY 10016 on the author's behalf.

THE COUNTRY CLUB by Douglas Carter Beane. Copyright © 2000, Douglas Carter Beane. Reprinted by permission of Glick and Weintraub, 1501 Broadway, Suite 2401, New York, NY 10036-5601 on the author's behalf.

COYOTE ON A FENCE by Bruce Graham. Copyright © 2000, Bruce Graham. Reprinted by permission of Harden-Curtis Associates, 850 Seventh Avenue, Suite 405, New York, NY 10019 on the author's behalf.

THE DIARY OF ANNE FRANK by Frances Goodrich and Albert Hackett. Newly adapted by Wendy Kesselman. Copyright © 2000, the Anne Frank-Fonds, Actors Fund of America, The Dramatists Guild, Inc., New Dramatists. Reprinted by permission of Douglas/Kopelman Agency, 393 West 49th Street, #5G, New York, NY 10019 on the author's behalf.